Race to the Potomac

LEE AND MEADE AFTER GETTYSBURG, JULY 4–14, 1863

by Bradley M. Gottfried and Linda I. Gottfried

EMERGING CIVIL WAR SERIES

Chris Mackowski, series editor
Cecily Nelson Zander, chief historian

The Emerging Civil War Series

offers compelling, easy-to-read overviews of some of the Civil War's most important battles and stories.

Recipient of the Army Historical Foundation's Lieutenant General Richard G. Trefry Award for contributions to the literature on the history of the U.S. Army

Also part of the Emerging Civil War Series:

The Aftermath of Battle: The Burial of the Civil War Dead by Meg Groeling

Don't Give an Inch: The Second Day at Gettysburg, July 2, 1863—From Little Round Top to Cemetery Ridge by Chris Mackowski, Kristopher D. White, and Daniel T. Davis

Fight Like the Devil: The First Day at Gettysburg, July 1, 1863 by Chris Mackowski, Kristopher D. White, and Daniel T. Davis

The Great Battle Never Fought: The Mine Run Campaign, November 26–December 2, 1863 by Chris Mackowski

The Last Road North: A Guide to the Gettysburg Campaign, 1863 by Robert Orrison and Dan Welch

The Most Desperate Acts of Gallantry: George A. Custer in the Civil War by Daniel T. Davis

Out Flew the Sabres: The Battle of Brandy Station, June 9, 1863 by Eric J. Wittenberg and Daniel T. Davis

Passing Through the Fire: Joshua Lawrence Chamberlain in the Civil War by Brian F. Swartz

Stay and Fight It Out: The Second Day at Gettysburg, July 2, 1863—Culp's Hill and the Northern End of the Battlefield by Kristopher D. White and Chris Mackowski

A Want of Vigilance: The Bristoe Station Campaign, October 9-19, 1863 by Bill Backus and Robert Orrison

Also by Bradley M. Gottfried and Linda I. Gottfried:

Hell Comes to Southern Maryland: The Story of Point Lookout Prison and Hammond General Hospital
Lincoln Comes to Gettysburg: The Creation of the Soldiers' National Cemetery and Lincoln's Gettysburg Address

Also by Bradley M. Gottfried:

Kearny's Own: The History of the First New Jersey Brigade in the Civil War
The Maps of First Bull Run
The Maps of Antietam
The Maps of Fredericksburg
The Maps of Gettysburg
The Maps of the Cavalry in the Gettysburg Campaign
The Maps of the Bristoe Station and Mine Run Campaigns
The Maps of the Wilderness
The Maps of Spotsylvania through Cold Harbor

For a complete list of titles in the Emerging Civil War Series, visit www.emergingcivilwar.com.

Race to the Potomac

LEE AND MEADE AFTER GETTYSBURG, JULY 4–14, 1863

by Bradley M. Gottfried and Linda I. Gottfried

EMERGING CIVIL WAR SERIES

Savas Beatie

California

First edition, first printing

ISBN-13: 978-1-61121-702-5 (paperback)
ISBN-13: 978-1-61121-703-2 (ebook)

Library of Congress Control Number: 2023045399

Names: Gottfried, Bradley M., author. | Gottfried, Linda I., author.
Title: Race to the Potomac: Lee and Meade after Gettysburg, July 4-14, 1863 / Bradley M Gottfried, Linda I Gottfried.
Other titles: Lee and Meade after Gettysburg, July 4-14, 1863
Description: El Dorado Hills, CA : Savas Beatie, [2024] | Series: Emerging Civil War series | Summary: "Even before the guns fell silent at Gettysburg, Robert E. Lee was preparing for the arduous task of getting his defeated army back safely into Virginia. It was an enormous, complex, and exceedingly dangerous undertaking, told here in exciting fashion"-- Provided by publisher.
Identifiers: LCCN 2023045399 | ISBN 9781611217025 (paperback) | ISBN 9781611217032 (ebook)
Subjects: LCSH: Virginia--History--Civil War, 1861-1865--Campaigns. | United States. Army of the Potomac. | Confederate States of America. Army of Northern Virginia. | United States--History--Civil War, 1861-1865--Campaigns. | Lee, Robert E. (Robert Edward), 1807-1870. | Meade, George Gordon, 1815-1872. | Gettysburg Campaign, 1863.
Classification: LCC E475.5 .G68 2024 | DDC 973.7/34--dc23/eng/20230928
LC record available at https://lccn.loc.gov/2023045399

Published by
Savas Beatie LLC
989 Governor Drive, Suite 102
El Dorado Hills, California 95762
Phone: 916-941-6896
sales@savasbeatie.com
www.savasbeatie.com

Savas Beatie titles are available at special discounts for bulk purchases in the United States by corporations, institutions, and other organizations. For more details, e-mail us at sales@savasbeatie.com or visit our website at www.savasbeatie.com for additional information.

Printed and bound in the United Kingdom

To Dean Shultz

A man who has devoted his life to the study of Gettysburg and has helped so many (including us) better understand the campaign. He truly earned the title of "Dean of the Gettysburg Campaign."

Table of Contents

Footnotes for this volume are available at
https://emergingcivilwar.com/publication/footnotes/

List of Maps

Maps by Hal Jespersen

Maps of daily movements originally published in
"Lee is Trapped and Must be Taken": Eleven Fateful Days after Gettysburg, July 4–14, 1863
Courtesy of Thomas J. Ryan and Richard R. Schaus

PHOTO CREDITS: Adams County Historical Society (achs); *Battles and Leaders of the Civil War* (b&l); *Our Country: A Household History for All Readers* by Benson J. Lossing (bjl); *A History of the United States of America* by Charles Morris (cm); *Frank Leslie's Weekly* (flw); Linda Gottfried (lg); Library of Congress (loc); New York Public Library (nypl); U.S. Army Heritage & Education Center (usahec)

For the Emerging Civil War Series

Theodore P. Savas, *publisher*

Sarah Keeney, *editorial consultant*

Veronica Kane, *production supervisor*

David Snyder, *copyeditor*

Patrick McCormick, *proofreader*

Chris Mackowski, *series editor and co-founder*

Cecily Nelson Zander, *chief historian*

Kristopher D. White, *emeritus editor*

Layout by Jess Maxfield
Maps by Hal Jespersen

Acknowledgments

The authors were assisted in their efforts by a number of individuals. First and foremost was Dean Shultz who carefully reviewed the manuscript and took the senior author on several tours of the escape/pursuit route.

Wally Heimbach, a former Gettysburg Licensed Battlefield Guide, who spent a day with the senior author in traveling the roads traversed by the soldiers after Gettysburg.

The staff of the Adams County Historical Society, particularly Andrew Dalton and Tim Smith, provided assistance in pulling pertinent photographs, many of which are used in this book.

Special thanks to Thomas J. Ryan and Richard R. Schaus for allowing us to use Hal Jespersen's wonderful maps from their seminal book, *"Lee is Trapped and Must be Taken"*. Hal also created a couple original maps for this book as well.

Cecily Zander did a great job of editing the book.

Finally, Chris Mackowski, the founder of the Emerging Civil War Series and its editor, provides encouragement and was always available for questions.

Seminary Ridge was the scene of heavy fighting on the afternoon of July 1. Lee consolidated his army here prior to his retreat on July 4. (lg)

$\mathcal{F}$oreword

BY ERIC J. WITTENBERG

Bradley L. Gottfried and Linda I. Gottfried have made an excellent contribution to the body of knowledge regarding the 10 days that followed the end of the battle of Gettysburg with their new book, *Race to the Potomac: Lee and Meade After Gettysburg, July 4–14, 1863*.

In the past 20 years, the events that occurred between the end of the battle of Gettysburg in the late afternoon of July 3, 1863, and the crossing of the Potomac River by Robert E. Lee's Army of Northern Virginia on July 14, 1863, have finally received the recognition that deserve. The first modern monograph, *Roads from Gettysburg*, was published by Rev. John Schildt in 1979 and paved the way for the rest of us who have documented these events, but his book is often overlooked. Next came Kent Masterson Brown's masterful 2005 monograph, *Retreat from Gettysburg: Lee, Logistics, and the Pennsylvania Campaign*. As the title suggests, Brown's book focuses on Confederate logistics during the retreat, and he makes a compelling argument that the Confederate invasion of Pennsylvania was really a giant raid seeking supplies for the Army of Northern Virginia to use.

Robert E. Lee made his headquarters in and around the Mary Thompson farmhouse upon his arrival on the battlefield. It is now preserved through the efforts of the American Battlefield Trust. (lg)

Next came my work, written along with J. David Petruzzi and Michael F. Nugent, *One Continuous Fight: The Retreat from Gettysburg and the Pursuit of Lee's Army of Northern Virginia, July 4–14, 1863*, published in 2008. We focused on the Union high command's decision-making and the intense cavalry fighting that occurred during the retreat. Our book was intended to complement Brown's work. In 2019, Thomas J. Ryan and Richard R. Schaus published *"Lee is Trapped and Must be Taken": Eleven Fateful Days after Gettysburg, July 4–14, 1863*, which further added to the body of knowledge concerning these events. The authors argue that Meade could have and should have done more, a conclusion I strongly disagree with.

That three major studies have been published in a span of fourteen years suggests that these events deserved much more study and analysis than prior historians gave them credit for. The reality is that both armies suffered dreadful losses at Gettysburg, with the Army of the Potomac's command structure having been devastated by the loss of three of its seven infantry corps commanders and the loss of the army's chief of staff. Those losses placed inexperienced—and, in two instances, unqualified—men in corps command and forced Cavalry Corps commander Alfred Pleasonton to also serve as de facto chief of staff until Maj. Gen. A. A. Humphreys accepted an appointment on July 10, 1863, to serve permanently in that position. Pleasonton lacked the ability to fill both roles simultaneously, and he permitted the cavalry to operate independently without much direction during the Confederate retreat from Gettysburg and the Union pursuit. That, in turn, permitted Robert E. Lee to seize the initiative, making it possible for his army to escape.

Both armies used thousands of wagons to transport ammunition, baggage and supplies, and the wounded. Destroying Lee's wagon train became the Union cavalry's objective after the battle. (loc)

It's important to note that there was no playbook for either Meade or Lee to follow. This situation was unprecedented: A defeated army trapped on the banks of a flooded river with no ability to escape but which had been re-supplied and occupied a stout defensive position. After the battle of Antietam on September 17, 1862, Lee's army retreated across the Potomac largely unmolested, save for a rearguard action at Shepherdstown Ford. Meanwhile, after defeats at Fredericksburg and Chancellorsville, the defeated Army of the Potomac was permitted to retreat unmolested. There simply was no parallel to the circumstances faced by George Gordon Meade and Robert E. Lee. Both had to make it up as they went.

Meade was further hindered by an inviolable order: He was to maintain his army interposed between Lee's army and Baltimore and Washington at all times. This meant that the Army of the Potomac could not take the most direct route to pursue Lee, and he also could not leave Gettysburg until he knew for certain that Lee intended to retreat across the Potomac River. These factors not only handcuffed Meade, they also helped shift the initiative away from the beleaguered Union commander to Lee.

Finally, Meade had only been in command of the army since June 28, 1863. He had fought and won a major battle on the soil of his home state, but his army suffered catastrophic losses in doing so, including major generals John F. Reynolds and Winfield S. Hancock, the two men he relied upon most. The Army of the Potomac's command structure was largely wrecked by heavy losses. Meade faced a nearly impossible task with an army that had been largely crippled at Gettysburg.

Given these constraints, I have concluded that George Meade did all that was possible given the circumstances. Perhaps you will draw a different conclusion, and I encourage you to learn more about these events in order to come to your own conclusions.

The Gottfrieds have written an excellent, concise-yet-comprehensive narrative of these events that serves as a strong primer to the retreat from Gettysburg. Filled with ample illustrations and good maps, *Race to the Potomac* provides a good basis for pursuing additional reading should you want to dig deeply into these events by reading the monographs previously mentioned. *Race to the Potomac* also includes five different driving tours that can be followed should you want to follow in the footsteps of the armies as they made their way to the banks of the Potomac River in July 1863. I am happy to recommend this fine work—another quality addition to the Emerging Civil War Series published by Savas-Beatie—as a gateway to deeper study or as a good overview for those satisfied with an introduction to these important events.

ERIC J. WITTENBERG *is an award-winning historian, blogger, speaker, and tour guide. His specialty is Civil War cavalry operations, and much of his work has focused on the Gettysburg Campaign.*

"Again, my dear general, I do not believe you appreciate the magnitude of the misfortune involved in Lee's escape—He was within your easy grasp, and to have closed upon him would, in connection with our other late successes, have ended the war—As it is, the war will be prolonged indefinitely."

— President Abraham Lincoln to Maj. Gen. George Gordon Meade

Prologue

Robert E. Lee returned to his headquarters around 1:00 a.m. on July 4, "riding alone, at a slow walk, and evidently wrapped in profound thought." That is how Brig. Gen. John Imboden recalled Lee after the crushing defeat of the Pickett-Pettigrew-Trimble Charge. When Imboden arrived at Lee's headquarters, the army chief was not present, so he found a tree nearby and probably slumbered under it. Imboden and his 2,100-man Northwestern Brigade arrived the day before, bone tired after their raid through what is now West Virginia, collecting livestock and supplies. They had been in the saddle since June 16, and welcomed a reprieve when arriving in Gettysburg around noon on July 3 to await further orders. Imboden was told to head over to Lee's quarters a few hours later.

The two armies, Lee's Army of Northern Virginia (72,000 men) and Maj. Gen. George Meade's Army of the Potomac (94,000 men) engaged in a death grapple for three days, from the morning of July 1 through the afternoon of July 3. The armies were worn out and the men craved rest and an end to the fighting. The casualties were staggering, totaling more than 46,000 overall.

John Imboden's wagon train of wounded Confederate soldiers almost immediately climbed the steep side of South Mountain leading to the Cashtown Pass. (lg)

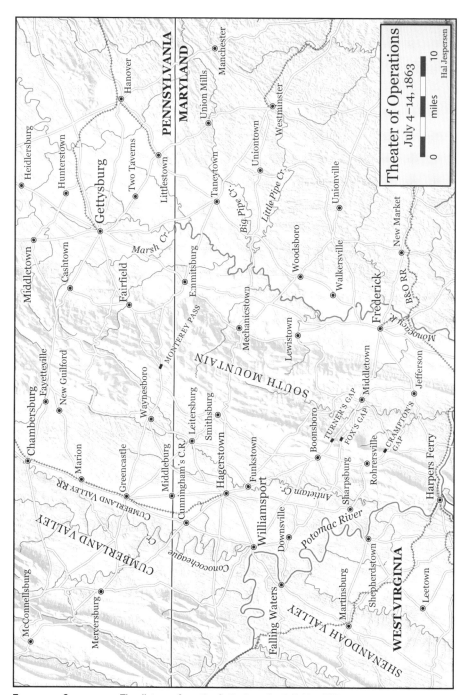

THEATER OF OPERATIONS—The distance from the Gettysburg battlefield to Williamsport, Maryland, on the Potomac River stretched over 40 miles, including the treacherous climb over South Mountain.

A New Jersey soldier recalled the "wreck of the battlestorm . . . broken caissons, dismounted guns, small arms bent and twisted by the storm or dropped and scattered by disabled hands; dead and bloated horses, torn and ragged equipments, and all the sorrowful wreck that the waves of battle leave at their ebb; and over all, hugging the earth like a fog, poisoning every breath, the pestilential stench of decaying humanity."

Meade later reported he considered a counterattack on July 3 against Lee's right flank. He demurred because of "the great length of the line, and the time required to carry these orders to the front, and the movements subsequently made, before the report given to me of the condition of the forces in the front and left, caused it to be so late in the evening as to induce me to abandon the assault which I had been contemplating."

Robert E. Lee's defeat at Gettysburg was a devastating setback for the Confederacy and for his own health. (loc)

Lee's Wagons Prepare for a Long Journey

Lee knew his army, while wounded, was still formidable and could fend for itself. He worried about the thousands of wagons loaded with the wounded, and the tons of supplies. Their vulnerability to hit-and-run attacks by Union cavalry demanded a head start to reach safety across the Potomac River. Hence, Lee bade Imboden to his headquarters. Upon seeing Imboden, Lee "reined in his jaded horse," and dismounted. "The effort to do so betrayed so much physical exhaustion that I hurriedly rose and stepped forward to assist him," Imboden recalled. Lee did not require assistance, but rested with his arm across the saddle, looking down at the ground. In the moonlight, Imboden recalled "an expression of sadness that I had never before seen upon his face."

Few men could have performed as well as Brig. Gen. John Imboden, tasked by Lee to shepherd the wagon train of misery to Williamsport, Maryland. (loc)

Imboden waited for his chieftain to speak, and when he did not, quietly said, "General, this has been a hard day on you." Lee responded in a voice "tremulous with emotion," characterizing Pickett's charge as "magnificent," but had they been supported, "the day would have been ours." Then Lee blurted out, almost in agony, "Too bad! Too bad! TOO BAD!"

He invited Imboden into his tent, where Lee revealed the cavalryman's mission: "As many of our poor wounded as possible must be taken home. I have sent for you, because your men and horses are fresh and in good condition, to guard and conduct our train back to Virginia." Lee understood the mission's difficulty, telling Imboden the duty would be "arduous,

Gruff and profane John Harman was just the man Lee needed to shepherd the reserve wagon train to Williamsport. (gmp)

responsible, and dangerous, for I am afraid you will be harassed by the enemy's cavalry." Lee then explained Imboden would cross the Potomac River at Williamsport, Maryland, and then continue onto Winchester, Virginia, and the network of medical facilities in the Shenandoah Valley. Imboden's mission was critical to the future of the Army of Northern Virginia, involving significant logistical challenges.

Wagons were a necessary evil of all armies. They transported ordnance (ammunition for small arms and artillery), supplies, ambulances, and the soldiers' personal effects. They affected how fast an army could move and where it could safely go. All told, Lee had about 5,000-6,000 wagons that, if placed end to end, stretched almost 50 miles.

Lee invaded southern Pennsylvania for several reasons. One of the most important included collecting supplies and livestock. His men captured thousands of head of livestock and tons of supplies. Soldiers serving in the army's quartermaster corps gathered supplies even as the Battle of Gettysburg raged. The materials were delivered to the "reserve train," which was situated between Fairfield and Cashtown, Pennsylvania, about eight miles from Gettysburg. When on the road, the train stretched between 15 to 20 miles. In addition to the reserve wagons, this train transported more than 5,000 cattle, almost the same number of sheep, and several thousand hogs. Major John Harman was responsible for the train's safety.

Thirty-nine-year-old Harman held various jobs before the Civil War, including newspaper editor and butcher. He was well-known in the Confederate army as a superb organizer and proficient swearer. He shared Imboden's angst over the retreat, for both were responsible for getting the precious trains to safety. Lieutenant General Richard Ewell, commander of the Confederate Second Corps, oversaw Harman's activities, summoning his subordinate to his headquarters at the end of the battle to receive his orders. As Harman departed, Ewell told him to "get that train safely across the Potomac or [I] want to see [your] face no more!"

Lee laid out two routes for his wagons. Harman would take the most direct route to Williamsport and the Potomac River. He would scale South Mountain just west of Fairfield, Pennsylvania and then make a rush into Maryland, passing through Leitersburg, Hagerstown, and finally ending at Williamsport. This route was shorter and more direct, but the portion over Jack's Mountain had sharp twists and turns, and Monterey Pass was steep and narrow. The Federals were also closest to this route, should they pursue. It could mean the loss of wagons, men, and captured supplies. Lee selected the longer, but easier and potentially safer Chambersburg Pike route for Imboden. The train's route headed north and west to Greenwood, New Franklin, Greencastle, and then into Maryland to Williamsport. Lee wanted to ensure the army's wounded men arrived safely, so they could recuperate in Southern hospitals and rejoin his ranks. Lee took pains during the battle to ensure both escape roads, Chambersburg Pike and Fairfield Road, remained in Confederate hands.

In addition to Imboden's and Harman's long trains, the wagons carrying the materials and supplies the infantry and artillery needed moved with their respective units. Many wounded would be transported via ambulances that accompanied their own corps. For example, the badly wounded Maj. Gen. John Bell Hood rode in a wagon following his infantry on Fairfield Road. The severely wounded who could not survive the journey, and those who could not fit into wagons, were left behind. Of the 1,300 wounded in Maj. Gen. Edward "Allegheny" Johnson's division, 446 were left to be captured and cared for by the Federals. The situation was even worse for Maj. Gen. Robert Rodes' division, leaving 760 wounded of the 1,600 disabled. Some in the wagons were in no condition to make the journey, and 28 men in Maj. Gen. Jubal Early's division died as their wagons headed the short distance to their jumping off points.

Meade Prepares to Follow Lee

Meade had many things on his mind—most important was caring for his own wounded army and, secondarily, following Lee toward the Potomac River. He could not allow Lee and his wagons to escape unscathed.

So began a desperate phase of the campaign, where one army attempted to escape and the other to prevent it.

The Two Armies Eye Each Other

CHAPTER ONE
JULY 4, 1863

A Busy Day for Lee

The day after the battle dawned overcast, threatening rain. Just after noon, the skies opened, and sheets of rain fell, soaking men and beasts and turning roads into mush. According to Gen. Imboden, "Horses and mules were blinded and maddened by the wind and water, and became almost unmanageable."

Lee's Army of Northern Virginia had battled for three days at Gettysburg. While they almost achieved success, it ultimately proved elusive. The army paid heavily for its second invasion of the United States, losing more than 23,000 men, including a third of its generals (17 of 52) with little to show for it. The army also faced a shortage of ammunition and supplies. Far from its supply base, it had to make do with what was available.

Not ready to cede victory, Lee shortened and straightened his line along Seminary Ridge beginning on the evening of July 3 and continuing into the following day. This meant vacating the town of

Travel on the modern macadam road to Fairfield is much smoother now than during the Civil War (see photo on page 3). (lg)

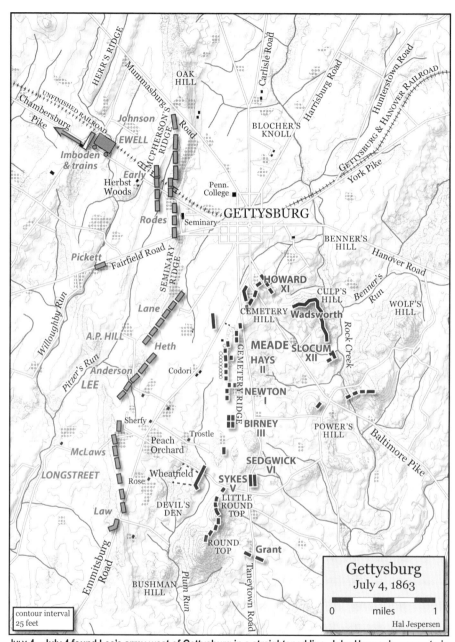

JULY 4—July 4 found Lee's army west of Gettysburg in a straightened line. John Harman's wagon train made good progress, its van reaching Williamsport by midnight. John Imboden's train got a late start but moved steadily along the Chambersburg Pike.

Gettysburg and placing his troops on Seminary Ridge, north toward Oak Hill and extending south to beyond Fairfield Road. Lieutenant Genereal A. P. Hill's Third Corps took up a position on the right of Lt. Gen. Richard Ewell's Second Corps, astride Fairfield

The dirt road leading to Fairfield often became muddy and rutted after a storm. Most of Lee's army used this route as it left the battlefield. (achs)

Road, with Lt. Gen. James Longstreet's First Corps extending the line to the south. Lee now awaited an attack on his strong position.

John West, a Texan in Hood's division, reported the men "threw up breastworks on the 4th with the hope that the enemy would leave his position in the mountains and attack us on the open plain, where we could have routed him and kept him in such confusion that a rally would have been impossible." He never forgot this July 4 as "we had no meat and a very little break for two days. Had not taken off our accouterments during the time, and the rain poured incessantly, so that the water on the level plain was two or three inches deep." Lee's entire infantry were engaged in building breastworks on July 4.

Around 30,000 wounded men lay between the two armies, unable to be moved from harm's way. Thousands more who had not survived the fight lay scattered among the wounded. While Lee awaited a possible attack on his strong position, he realized the time had come to consider getting his army back to Virginia. The task would not be easy, as there was 50 miles between Lee and safety.

Union prisoners, numbering 5,000, posed another logistical issue. Lee wrote to Meade on July 4 suggesting a prisoner exchange. Meade also held thousands of Confederate prisoners. The cartel for exchanging captured men had ceased to exist in May 1863, so Meade could only reply, "it is not in my power to accede to the proposed arrangement." Lee pondered his

Both armies used signal stations to observe the enemy's movements and convey this information, usually via flags, to army headquarters. (loc)

options and paroled about 1,500 Union troops, leaving him with 4,000 Federal prisoners of war. These men became part of Lee's retreat. Major General George Pickett's division, now reduced to the size of a brigade, was responsible for guarding the prisoners. Lee put the prisoners in the middle of his retreating column. The prisoners were in poor shape—most had not eaten for several days, and were exhausted. Each received a half pint of flour on July 4, but rain prevented them from cooking it; some also received small amounts of beef.

A Busy Day for Meade

Appointed to army command only three days before the battle of Gettysburg, Maj. Gen. George Meade effectively handled his army and gained a major victory. He would lead the army through the remainder of the war, but would be subordinated by Lincoln and, later, by U. S. Grant. (loc)

George Gordon Meade spent July 4 on a myriad of tasks. Although the enemy appeared beaten, they remained a dangerous foe, potentially ready to strike again. His signal stations reported the enemy had vacated Gettysburg during the night, suggesting a retreat. Meade did not believe this was enough information, so he waited for additional intelligence. He ordered strong reconnaissance parties to probe Lee's lines, determining its location and strength. Meade communicated with Washington, assessing the condition of his units, and putting his men to work, burying those dead behind Union lines. This task expanded to include Confederate dead, beginning on July 5.

The need to respond to a Confederate retreat weighed on Meade, and he devoted some energy to developing a plan, should Lee decide to fall back to Virginia. Meade wrote to Maj. Gen. Darius Couch, commander of the Department of the Susquehanna, around 10:00 p.m. on July 3. Meade did not believe Lee planned an attack but was unsure of the next moves of the Army of Northern Virginia. It could move to South Mountain, where Lee could fortify and await an attack, or continue retreating to Virginia via the Cumberland Valley. In any case, Meade wanted Couch to be ready to support the Army of the Potomac. If Lee headed for South Mountain, Meade would incorporate Couch's men into his command; if the Confederate leader opted for the Cumberland Valley, Meade wanted Couch to pursue him as rapidly as possible. Couch immediately ordered Brig. Gen. William "Baldy" Smith's 10,000-man division, at Carlisle, Pennsylvania, to begin moving south.

Couch cautioned Meade to temper his expectations for Smith's troops: "one-half are very worthless, and 2,000 [enemy] cavalry, with a battery, can capture the whole party in an open country. This is why I put them in or near the mountains; there they could do service." Meade wrote to Brig. Gen. William French, whose division occupied Frederick, Maryland, on July 4, to move north, occupying the South Mountain passes through Maryland, while Smith's men headed for Pennsylvania.

Many of Meade's officers, and those in the rank and file, disagreed with their commander's decision not to attack Lee's position on Seminary Ridge. Maj. Gen. Carl Schurz, commanding a division in the XI Corps, believed a full-scale attack on Lee's positions after the bloody repulse of the Pickett-Pettigrew-Trimble Charge could have made Meade's victory even more decisive. He felt the situation demanded "instant resolution." A young Massachusetts fifer thought Meade "seemed as afraid [of Lee] after the battle as before." A Confederate newspaper correspondent had a different perspective. Although Lee tried to bait Meade into an attack by sending forward a strong skirmish line, the correspondent considered the Union commander to "be well aware of the strength of his own position and the madness of attacking Lee."

George Meade's victorious army was in rough shape. Three of its corps, the I, III, and XI, were wrecked, and two others, the II and V, sustained heavy losses. Only the VI and XII Corps were in fairly good shape. In addition to losing over 23,000 men, the officer corps lost heavily. One of Meade's corps commanders was dead, and two others severely wounded. Meade was also concerned about the dearth of supplies for the men, particularly food and ammunition, stemming from the destruction of the North Central and Hanover railroads by the Confederates. He was forced to rely on the Western Maryland Railroad, which delivered goods from Baltimore to Westminster, Maryland, about 25 miles by road to Gettysburg. Meade had one advantage over Lee in the logistics department. Brigadier General Henry Haupt, head of the Union's Military Railway Department, realized the Hanover-Gettysburg Railroad provided the speediest succor. The Army of Northern Virginia had

Major General Darius Couch rose quickly through the ranks to become commander of the Union II Corps at the battle of Fredericksburg. A quarrel with army commander, Maj. Gen. Joseph Hooker, after Chancellorsville caused Couch to seek reassignment, and he was subsequently appointed head of the Department of the Susquehanna during the Gettysburg Campaign. (loc)

Brigadier General Herman Haupt was a railroader extraordinaire. He initially refused the rank of brigadier general as he wanted to continue to work independently. A fight with Washington about the nature of his appointment caused him to leave the service in September 1863. (loc)

destroyed many of its bridges, so putting it back into action was daunting, but Haupt was up to the task.

After the Army of the Potomac's countless prior defeats, Meade felt a congratulatory communication was in order. He lauded his troops for their tenacity and looked to the army "for greater efforts to drive from our soil every vestige of the presence of the invaders." The phrase might have seemed innocent, but President Abraham Lincoln exploded when he read it, exclaiming, "Drive the invaders from our soil. My God! Is that all!" Some of Meade's men shared Lincoln's exasperation. A soldier in the 13th Massachusetts wrote, "we could not escape the impression that it [the three days of battle at Gettysburg] was a repetition of Antietam, for in both cases the enemy was granted 'leave to withdraw at a time when it could have had little expectation of the exercise of so benignant a privilege." Although Meade's communication heartened many of his troops, they probably preferred a good hot meal and an end to torrential rains. They took pains to keep their rifles serviceable by attempting to maintain dry barrels and ammunition. Men of the 118th Pennsylvania fixed bayonets to their rifles and thrust them into the ground so the rainwater would not dampen the barrels. Keeping their powder dry was a challenging issue.

An ecstatic Abraham Lincoln closely followed the events of the Gettysburg Campaign, but his delight turned to frustration because he believed Meade could have pursued Lee's army more aggressively. (loc)

Meade also spent considerable time on July 4 pondering his options regarding Lee. He had first to make sure the Army of Northern Virginia was actually withdrawing, and if so, that the Federals were not being lured into a trap. Assuming Lee was retreating to Virginia, he had several options. He could do nothing, remaining on the battlefield and licking his wounds. Major General George McClellan had done this after the battle of Antietam and was removed from command of the Army of the Potomac. Meade could follow the path of Lee's beaten army, hoping to catch up and deliver a fatal blow. He knew Lee must traverse mountain gaps to get into the Cumberland Valley. Lee could stop and use the high ground to defeat the Union Army. Marching behind a defeated army exposed it to irksome delays, broken down wagons, wounded men who couldn't keep up, and discarded equipment. The best approach was a parallel move toward the enemy's destination. With haste and some luck, Meade's army could reach the endpoint before Lee, or at the very least, cause it to speed up, furthering its disintegration.

Meade believed Lee was heading for Williamsport, the closest Potomac River crossing point. Moving south toward Williamsport meant that Meade's army could remain between Lee and Baltimore and Washington, so the Confederate Army could not change tack toward one or the other. Time and distance were not on Meade's side. There were 64 miles between the Army of the Potomac and Williamsport, compared with the 44-mile march Lee faced.

Meade decided on a march for Williamsport by 1:30 p.m. on July 4. He wrote to Gen. Couch, "as soon as it can be definitely ascertained that Lee is retiring into the [Cumberland] valley, I shall move rapidly in a southern direction." He wrote Gen. William Smith that he intended to move via Emmitsburg and Middletown after Lee's army. It required time for Meade to uncoil his army and begin marching after Lee, so he ordered Maj. Gen. Alfred Pleasonton, his cavalry chief, to harass Lee, and hopefully reach Williamsport before the enemy.

Meade then ordered the First Cavalry Division under Brig. Gen. John Buford to ride from Westminster to Frederick and then to Williamsport. This route allowed Buford to operate in the Cumberland Valley, Lee's presumed route to the Potomac River. The Third Cavalry Division, under Brig. Gen. Judson Kilpatrick, would ride to Emmitsburg, Maryland, collecting Col. Pennock Huey's brigade (Gregg's Second Cavalry Division), cross South Mountain, protecting Meade's left flank, and attack enemy wagon trains as conditions permitted. Brigadier General David Gregg's Second Division split up: Col. Irvin Gregg headed over to the Cashtown Pass to worry Lee's right flank, and Col. John McIntosh's brigade remained with Sedgwick's VI Corps, harassing the enemy's rearguard, after scouting near Emmitsburg

Although he had won a victory over Lee, Meade remained uncomfortable making important command decisions alone. Given that he had commanded the army for less than a week, Meade's discomfort could be read as a commander acting properly. He called a war council with his corps commanders at his

Major General Alfred Pleasonton commanded the Army of the Potomac's mounted arm during Lee's two invasions of the North. Upon George Meade's appointment to army command, Pleasonton was relegated to essentially a staff officer and played only an indirect role in his cavalry's actions after Gettysburg. (loc)

John Irvin Gregg commanded a cavalry brigade in the cavalry division of his cousin David Gregg. He saw considerable action at Gettysburg and during the remainder of the Civil War. (usahec)

Ambulances, not wagons, were designed to carry the wounded, but the sheer number of wounded forced Lee to use many different types of wagons to get his men back to Virginia. (loc)

headquarters on the army's extreme right during the evening of July 4. He asked the assembled generals four questions:

1. *"Shall the army remain [at Gettysburg?].*
Most believed the army should take no action until it was definitely ascertained Lee was indeed retreating.

2. *"If we remain, shall we assume the offensive?"*
None favored gambling their gains on an attack against Lee.

3. *"Do you deem it expedient to move toward Williamsport through Emmitsburg?"*
Most agreed a parallel course was most expedient.

4. *"Shall we pursue the enemy if he is retreating on his direct line of retreat?"*
None voted affirmatively on this last question.

Meade later explained why he sought counsel from his senior lieutenants: "I had just assumed command of the army, and felt that it was due to myself to have the opinions of high officers before I took action on matters which involved such momentous issues."

Historians are unsettled about when Lee decided to retreat. He probably knew it was his best option as early as the afternoon of July 3, but it was not a light decision. The fact that Lee was more than 40 miles from the Potomac River and the relative safety of Virginia made this retreat more complex than the first time Lee moved north in 1862.

The mission was complicated by the thousands of wagons, loaded with wounded and tons of supplies secured in Pennsylvania. John Harman's trains would depart first, followed by Ewell's ambulances and wagons, and then A. P. Hill's Third Corps (and his wagons), closest to Fairfield Road in the center of Lee's defensive line.

Hill was tasked with marching his men in the darkness to Monterey Pass through South Mountain, selecting the "strongest ground for defense toward the east" to place the corps in a position to fend off any attack. James Longstreet's First Corps followed Hill, and Richard Ewell's Second Corps brought up the rear. This route left Gettysburg on Fairfield Road to the village of Fairfield. It then continued to Waynesboro, Hagerstown, and Williamsport, where wagons and men would cross the river on a pontoon bridge.

Stuart sent two cavalry brigades under Brig. Gen. Wade Hampton and Brig. Gen. Fitz Lee to guard Imboden's wagons, and two others (Brig. Gen. Beverly Robertson's and Brig. Gen. William Jones's) kept open Fairfield Road and other important roads leading from it. The remaining brigades (Col. William Chambliss's and Col. Milton Ferguson's) guarded the left flank. The trains initially stretched over 50 miles, making it almost impossible to protect the line from marauding enemy troops.

Brigadier General Wade Hampton may have been the wealthiest man in the South. A natural leader of men, he would assume command of Jeb Stuart's cavalry corps after the latter's death in May 1864. (loc)

Lee's Retreat Begins the Union Cavalry Pursuit

CHAPTER TWO
JULY 4, 1863

John Harman put his immense wagon train on the road at 3:00 a.m. on July 4. The wagons assembled near Cashtown, eight miles northwest of Gettysburg. Their journey would take them first to Fairfield, almost due south, then west and south into Maryland, and finally to Williamsport. The passage over South Mountain posed Harman's biggest challenge. The road was steep and narrow through Monterey Pass, and his train was vulnerable to an attack by Union cavalry while traversing this area. Harman did not have many protectors during his journey to the Potomac River. Initially, Robertson's and "Grumble" Jones' cavalry brigades guarded the vital roads west and south of Gettysburg that led to Fairfield and Emmitsburg. Once Harman passed this point, he could rely on only the 1st Maryland Cavalry Battalion and the four Napoleon guns of Capt. William Tanner's Virginia battery—scant protection for such an important train.

Harman's reserve train's last wagon left Fairfield at 1:00 p.m. on July 4. In ten hours, the train had covered a mere eight miles. Ewell's Second Corps

Many of John Imboden's wagons began their journey along the Chambersburg Pike (the current Route 30) near the Herr Tavern, which was built in 1815. (lg)

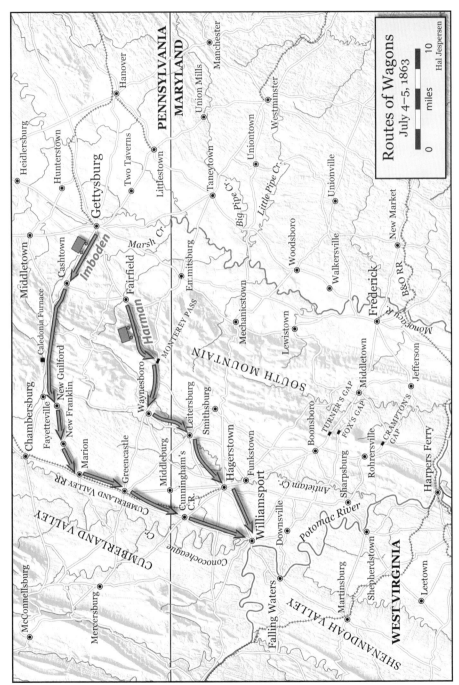

ROUTES OF WAGONS—Lee selected two routes for his vital wagon trains. John Harman's reserve train, filled with supplies, took the more direct route from Fairfield to Hagerstown and then on to Williamsport. John Imboden's wagons, filled with the wounded, took a northern route toward the Potomac River in an attempt to keep it out of harm's way.

wagons, strung out over 20 miles, fell in behind Harman's. Rodes' wagons joined the caravan first, followed by Early's, as Johnson's brought up the rear. As they passed, Ewell's ambulances joined the column. Once on the road and out of Fairfield, the train made better time, but posed a greater challenge for Harman, whose column now stretched nearly 40 miles.

The wagons in Harman's van approached Hagerstown, Maryland, around 9:00 p.m. The rear of the train still extended back beyond South Mountain. The head of the train carried on to Williamsport, arriving at midnight.

Back at Cashtown, Imboden realized his immense wagon train was still being assembled and would not be ready to roll until late afternoon. It took considerable time for the wounded to be carefully loaded from their field hospitals and then head to the assembling point. Because of inadequate ambulance numbers, converted Conestoga wagons composed most of Imboden's train. They were built to carry barrels and supplies, so they were long, usually 18 feet, and spring-less. Human comfort was not factored into their design. While the exact number of wounded carried by Imboden's trains is unknown, residents along the way estimated they totaled as many as 12,000 men.

There were not enough wagons to accommodate the injured troops, so they scoured the area for any wheeled vehicle, even buggies. The badly wounded or those that could not find space on a wagon were left behind. Some wounded walked beside the wagons. A few empty wagons followed the train to replace those that had broken down, and for those who could not continue the journey on foot. Bringing up the rear (in front of the cavalry) toiled several hundred horses, which had broken down during the campaign and were being returned to Virginia for rest and medical attention.

Deteriorating weather hampered efforts to assemble the trains. "The rain fell in blinding sheets," wrote Imboden. "During the storm, wagons, ambulances, and artillery carriages by hundreds—nay, by thousands were assembling in the fields along the road from Gettysburg to Cashtown, in one confused and apparently inextricable mass."

Imboden received written orders that morning, along with a large envelope addressed to President

Brigadier General Beverly Robertson was considered by many to be an incompetent cavalry brigade commander. He left the Army of Northern Virginia after Gettysburg to command a South Carolina military district. (loc)

Newly minted division commander Maj. Gen. Dorsey Pender led his unit for the first time at Gettysburg. The thigh wound he sustained on July 2 was not thought to be mortal, but infection, combined with the rigors of the wagon ride to the Potomac River, killed this promising young leader. (loc)

Brigadier General Alfred Scales received his third wound of the war at Gettysburg. He quickly returned to the army, participating in the Overland Campaign and part of the Petersburg Campaign. His unhealed wounds forced him to take leave of the army, so he was not present at Appomattox Court House. (loc)

Jefferson Davis. The orders were explicit: Turn off Chambersburg Pike at Greenwood, but keep scouts to the left, toward Waynesboro. A scouting party would be sent to hold Hagerstown when the column reached Greencastle. Once at the Potomac River, Imboden would post additional scouts at Hagerstown and Boonsboro.

Imboden's 17-mile-long train received several units to protect it: his brigade, two of Maj. Gen. J. E. B. Stuart's cavalry brigades, and 24 cannon in three batteries (Washington Artillery, Capt. James Hart's horse battery, and his own battery under Capt. James McClanahan). The column finally left the staging area near Cashtown at 4:00 p.m. and headed west toward Chambersburg with the 18th Virginia Cavalry and two guns from McClanahan's battery at the lead. Imboden remained behind, assembling troops and artillery, which he placed along the train at quarter-mile intervals. Two cavalry brigades, Brig. Gen. Fitz Lee's and Brig. Gen. Wade Hampton's (under Col. Laurence Baker), supported by their artillery, brought up the rear of the column.

The first wagon in the train carried two generals: Maj. Gen. Dorsey Pender and Brig. Gen. Alfred Scales. Other generals, such as John Hood, who sustained a serious arm wound when an artillery shell exploded over his head on July 2, and Gen. Wade Hampton, who took two saber blows to his head and a bullet to his hip on July 3, were in one of Harman's wagons. Hood recalled, ". . . Hampton, so badly wounded that he was unable to sit up, whereas I could not lie down." They were fortunate to be placed in a wagon with springs that helped cushion the ride on the rutted road. Most of the other wounded men were not so fortunate. By comparison, Pender and Scales suffered from a lack of cushioning, and Imboden thought the difficult trip "cost poor [Brig. Gen. Dorsey] Pender his life." After crossing the Potomac River, most of the wounded continued their journey to hospitals in Staunton, Virginia, almost 200 uncomfortable miles from Gettysburg.

Imboden's wagons headed north and then west to the Chambersburg Pike (modern Pennsylvania Route 30), continuing west in the pouring rain, which turned the country roads into mush. Once the train reached the Pike, the macadamized road offered relief from the mud, speeding travel along. A Confederate cavalryman heard "a low rumbling sound . . . resembling distant thunder, except that it was continuous." The men could not understand what it was until they "rose to our feet and saw a long line of wagons with their white covers moving . . . along the Chambersburg Road." The wagons' canvas covers were no match for the rain, and according to Imboden, "the wounded men lying upon the naked boards . . . were drenched."

The wagons congregated in the roads and fields from Herr Tavern to Cashtown, where Gen. Imboden made his headquarters. He left the town after dark (perhaps as late as 8:00 p.m.), riding as fast as he could to the head of the column. His orders were to keep moving with "no halt for any cause whatever. If an accident should happen to any vehicle, it was immediately to be put out of the road and abandoned" after the wounded were transferred to other wagons. Civilians along the rolling train of misery recalled teamsters removing dead bodies from the wagons, leaving them along the side of the roads to create space for the wagon-less wounded.

It took Imboden four hours to gain the front of the column, and he forever remembered the "heart-rending wails of agony" from the wounded. He estimated only a hundred may have received any medical attention before being placed in the wagons, and few had eaten in the previous 36 hours. "Their torn and bloody clothing, matted and hardened, was rasping the tender, inflamed, and still oozing wounds." Body fluids glued some of the men to the floorboards. Imboden sympathized for the men who lay in the wagons without straw to cushion them. "The jolting was enough to have killed strong men, if long exposed to it." The teamsters whipped their teams to hasten the journey, and among cries and shrieks could be heard, "Oh God! Why can't I die!" among other pleadings and oaths.

As the night wore on, a cavalryman recalled how the "rain fell in sheets and vivid flashes of lightning and so dark we could not see our hands an inch from our eyes when there was no lightning. The roar of the waters and heavy bursting thunder, the cries of the wounded and dying soldiers made it awful." The teamsters had difficulty navigating the storm, but it was a mixed blessing, for it reduced the probability of attacks by pursuing Union cavalrymen.

John B. Hood lost the use of his left arm at Gettysburg. He returned to the army only to sustain a wound at the battle of Chickamauga that required amputation of his right leg. (loc)

Although not as well-known as Alfred Pleasonton's other two cavalry commanders, Brig. Gen. David Gregg was a solid division commander whose actions at the battle of Gettysburg were overshadowed by Brig. Gen. George Custer's exploits. (loc)

The aggressive Brig. Gen. Hugh Judson Kilpatrick played a major role throughout the Gettysburg Campaign. Known as "Kill Cavalry," he was later transferred to command a cavalry division in George Thomas's Army of the Cumberland. (loc)

The Union Cavalry Begins Its Pursuit

The Union cavalry had evolved considerably since the beginning of the war, when it was ill-used, poorly equipped, out-maneuvered, and out-fought by its Confederate counterpart. Under the command of Maj. Gen. Alfred Pleasonton, the cavalry arm had grown to almost 12,000 troopers, organized into a corps of three divisions. The First Division was commanded by Brig. Gen. John Buford, a tough and effective commander, who tenaciously held the high ground west of Gettysburg on the morning of July 1, until reinforced by I Corps infantry. Buford could have pulled his exhausted troopers back, but he remained on the battlefield, fighting and scouting through the first day's battle and into the second.

Brigadier General David Gregg, also a seasoned commander, oversaw the Second Division. His division had arrived at Gettysburg on July 2, and held an important portion of a Confederate infantry division in place, so it could not attack Culp's Hill that night. The following day, Gregg's men took on Jeb Stuart and the Confederate cavalry, attempting to reunite with Lee's army. This resulted in a resounding Union victory, engineered in large part by Gregg with help from Brig. Gen. George Custer's command.

The Third Division was a bit of a question mark. It had been newly transferred to Pleasonton's command from the Washington defenses, and was placed under the command of Brig. Gen. Hugh Judson Kilpatrick, who had a mixed record as a brigade commander. Sometimes called "Kill Cavalry" for his exploits, it was thought he cared more about gaining glory for himself than about his men. Now he had something to prove to Pleasonton and others, and relished his opportunities at Gettysburg. After the repulse of the Pickett-Pettigrew-Trimble Charge, Kilpatrick tested the Confederate right flank, gaining nothing but the loss of many men, including one of his brigadier generals, Elon Farnsworth.

A Union signal station on the battlefield reported a large wagon train moving from Gettysburg in a southwest direction. The signalmen could not know these wagons probably constituted Harman's reserve train. After consulting with Meade, Pleasonton ordered his cavalry commanders to gain the enemy's rear, disrupt his line of communication, and harass and annoy them as much as possible. Only Gregg and Kilpatrick were initially available for this activity, as Buford's men were refitting at Westminster, Maryland. They joined the pursuit later.

This ambitious Kilpatrick received his orders on the morning of July 4: move to Emmitsburg and, with one of Gregg's brigades, destroy a "heavy train of wagons [Harman's train] . . . moving on the road to Hagerstown" and then to "operate on the enemy's rear and flanks." It was just the assignment Kilpatrick craved. General Gregg did not have this opportunity as his division was broken apart, and its brigades sent on different assignments. Col. John McIntosh's First Brigade would follow Lee's rearguard toward Fairfield. Col. Pennock Huey's Second Brigade, which had already been detached, would be further delayed in reuniting with the division as it was attached to Kilpatrick's division. Only Col. Irvin Gregg's Third Brigade remained directly under Gen. Gregg, and headed after Imboden's trains.

This period photograph shows the Chambersburg Turnpike as it winds its way toward Cashtown. (achs)

Kilpatrick immediately informed his men of their mission, which involved separation from the rest of the army and operating independently against the enemy. Each man would carry three days' rations and prepare to move out immediately. The troopers were on the road by 10:00 a.m. on July 4. "Not even a heavy thunder shower that came up soon after we got on the road, did not dampen the ardor of any in the division," exaggerated one of Kilpatrick's troopers. Others recalled the ride differently. "The wind blows furious, which makes the rain doubly unpleasant," wrote one. Another recalled the storm as the most furious they had ever experienced. The wind and rain probably dampened any enthusiasm the men may have harbored before mounting their horses.

Kilpatrick reached Emmitsburg at 3:00 p.m., picked up Col. Pennock Huey's brigade, and continued toward Monterey Pass through South Mountain. Along the way, the column encountered Confederate cavalrymen, driving them away. Custer's brigade led the pursuit. A local farmer, C. H. Buhrman, reported seeing Confederate wagons making their way through Monterey Pass along the Maria Furnace Road and brought this information to Kilpatrick. Sensing an opportunity, Kilpatrick hastened his command up the mountain.

The Third Division's ride up South Mountain was treacherous. "On my left was a deep ravine, on my right a steep, rugged mountain, and a road too narrow to reverse even a gun. To add to this unpleasant position, it was raining in torrents," reported Kilpatrick." Edward Paul, a New York Times reporter, elaborated on the climb:

Entitled "Saying Goodbye," this sketch depicted the wagon train of misery, which began with considerable hope for the well-being of the wounded before, sadly, earning its enduring name of woe. (b&l)

> *Imagine a long column of cavalry winding its way up the mountain side . . . which sloped at an angle of thirty degrees just wide enough for four horses to march abreast—on one side a deep abyss and on the other an impassable barrier…and so dark as literally not to be able to see one's own hand if placed within a foot of the organs of vision; the whole command, both men and animals, worn out with fatigue and loss of sleep.*

The gap was mostly undefended because most of Robertson's and Jones's cavalry brigades were still in the column's rear. Additional help was on the way, but would it arrive in time to ward off Kilpatrick's troopers? Unlike the First and Third Corps wagons, which traveled within their infantry columns and were well protected, Lee allowed Harman's reserve train and the Second Corps' wagons and ambulances to head west without much protection. When Ewell realized the danger, he immediately dispatched the Second Corps unit closest to Fairfield Road, which happened to be the hapless North Carolina brigade of Brig. Gen. Alfred Iverson. The unit was the first encountered by Col. Abner Smead, the Second Corps Inspector, who found it resting near the Lutheran Theological Seminary. The brigade was devastated by its attack on a strong Union position on the afternoon of July 1, and was a shadow of its former self. Smead ordered the brigade forward, so men quickly collected their belongings at 2:00 p.m., and with bayonets fixed at right shoulder shift, began their expedited march along Fairfield Road toward Monterey Pass, some of it at the double-quick.

Lee's Army Begins Its Long Journey

With his pair of wagon trains pushing ahead, Lee put his infantry columns on the road. A.P. Hill's Third Corps, in the center of Lee's line closest to Fairfield Road, vacated its position on Seminary Ridge first. It began its march toward the Potomac River around 5:00 p.m. on July 4. Major General Richard Anderson's division led the column, falling in behind Harman's long wagon train. Because of the importance of keeping the roads open for wheeled vehicles and the ever-deepening mud, the infantry marched in the fields adjacent to the roads. Anderson explained in his report, "Late in the evening, I received orders to draw off the division as soon as it became dark, and take the road to Fairfield." Once in the mountains, Hill's corps were to locate a good defensive position to defend the train if Meade decided to aggressively pursue Lee's column. Lee decided on a slow, and if necessary, a fighting retreat.

Brigadier General Ambrose "Rans" Wright was an attorney prior to the war. He enlisted as a private and rose through the ranks to become a dependable brigade commander in Lee's army. (loc)

Lee's long wagon train, the weather, and the men's poor physical and emotional condition all conspired to slow the retreat. The roads and fields quickly turned into muddy quagmires, further slowing the march. A soldier called it "a vast moving panorama of misery," while another explained that they were "up to our knees in mud and water all night. It was impossible to preserve the company organization in such darkness and difficult marching. The men would halloo out the names of their companies in order to keep together." The slow eight-mile march to Fairfield took the head of Anderson's division six hours to complete. Brigadier General Ambrose Wright's brigade, in Anderson's van, finally reached Fairfield around midnight, but there was no end to the march. The Georgians continued their march up the mountainside to help Iverson's men protect the wagons.

Cavalry Clashes as Lee Moves South

CHAPTER THREE
JULY 5, 1863

The Cavalry Fight at Monterey Pass

Judson Kilpatrick's long column of horsemen struggled up Monterey Pass on the Waynesboro-Emmitsburg Turnpike at about 10:00 p.m. on July 4. The 5th Michigan Cavalry of George Custer's brigade led the column. The men had been on the road for about 12 hours, and many were asleep in their saddles.

Only a couple 1st Maryland (CSA) Cavalry Battalion companies were spread around South Mountain to protect Monterey Pass. The ninety men of Company B under Capt. George Emack, with one gun of Capt. William Tanner's battery (with only five rounds in its ammunition chest), were positioned near the pass. Another portion of the 1st Maryland Cavalry Battalion, Company D, occupied the west side of the mountain, guarding against an attack from the direction of Waynesboro. These two units were no match for Kilpatrick's three brigades, composed of over 4,500 men, supported by three batteries, making their way up the mountainside.

Most of Lee's army, and a portion of Meade's, traveled through the town of Fairfield, just west of Gettysburg. The road through the town was not paved as it is today. (lg)

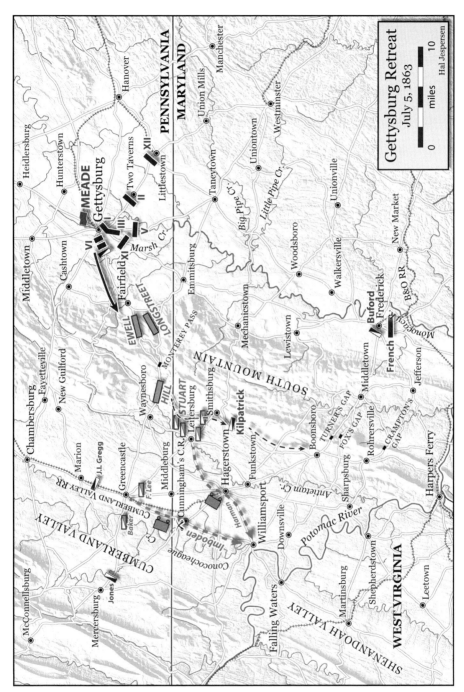

JULY 5—Union cavalry regularly attacked the rapidly moving Confederate trains heading for Williamsport, Maryland. After the devastating attacks on Harman's wagons at Monterey Pass and Leitersburg, Southern cavalry commander Jeb Stuart caught up with Kilpatrick's cavalry at Smithsburg. The day also saw Lee putting his infantry on the road, followed by the Union VI Corps.

What happened when the two parties clashed in the ensuing hours is open to debate. Intense darkness, driving rain, and fatigue caused accounts to differ wildly. Historians will probably never know exactly what happened around Monterey Pass during the night of July 4–5.

What is clear is that Kilpatrick could not have known the rear of Harman's reserve train had passed through Monterey Pass ahead of him. By the time the Union officer arrived at Monterey Pass, Harman's lead wagons had reached Hagerstown, after more than 18 hours of travel. Ewell's trains, with Rodes' divisional wagons in the van, were behind Harman's reserve train, crossing the mountain pass.

Confederate commander Emack positioned around 20 men along the pike, possibly at a curve in the road, stationing the remainder of his men behind them, further up the mountain. Emack decided to halt the portion of the train that had not yet reached the pass. Help was on the way, as Gen. William Jones sent portions of the 6th Virginia Cavalry and 4th North Carolina Cavalry forward to assist. The roughly 200 men added to Emack's unit were no match against Kilpatrick. General Jones rode ahead of his men, and when he saw the halted wagons, he got them moving again, much to Emack's chagrin.

Experienced teamsters were the lifeblood of the Confederate wagon trains. Many were slaves who followed their masters into the army. (loc)

As Kilpatrick's troopers approached Emack's skirmish line, the latter opened fire, as did the lone Confederate Napoleon cannon, firing rounds of canister into the darkness. A Michigander recalled the rounds went "over our heads, through the trees and down the mountain . . . whether [it] is shot, shell, grape & canister, shrapnel, or the remnants of an old blacksmith shop, I could not tell by the sound."

Emack added to the confusion by sending eight of his mounted men on a desperate charge into the van of the Union column. The darkness disguised the attackers, so the Michiganders could not tell whether a handful of men or a full regiment was attacking

Now only a road trace, Maria Furnace Road was an important thoroughfare during the Civil War, providing a direct route from Fairfield to Monterey Pass. (lg)

them. They halted and then reeled toward the rear in panic. The *New York Times* correspondent wrote, "the first squadron of the Fifth broke, fell back upon the second and broke that—but there was no such thing as running back a great ways on that road; it was jammed with men and horses."

Emack fell back about 200 yards, set up a skirmish line, and waited. It took another hour for Custer's men, at the head of the column, to attempt another push against the unseen enemy. During that time, the anxious wagoneers on Maria Furnace Road, just beyond the fighting, whipped their horses to put as much distance between them and Monterey Pass. Emack's men waited until Custer's men were a handful of paces away before opening fire, accompanied by the boom of Tanner's lone cannon. By moving about and hiding behind different trees, Emack's men gave the impression of being more numerous than they were. Their deception prompted Kilpatrick to dismount a company of the 18th Pennsylvania Cavalry to flank Emack and Tanner's cannon, without success.

Captain Emack fell back to a third position near the Monterey Hotel, a popular antebellum roadside stop. Custer reorganized his men and sent them forward a third time. One of his troopers accidentally stepped on a Marylander in the darkness and was quickly killed as the rest of Emack's men opened fire, again sending the Michiganders to the rear. Emack pulled his men back to the top of the pass, just east of Maria Furnace Road, to reorganize. He remained between Kilpatrick and the wagon train.

General Jones arrived and observed the gallant Marylanders slowly retreat from the pass. He encouraged Emack to continue fighting, promising to bring up his 6th Virginia Cavalry to assist, since hundreds of wagons were in imminent danger. Jones ordered his staff officers and couriers to dismount and join Emack's small but determined band.

Colonel Pennock Huey's cavalry brigade had the misfortune of missing the battle of Gettysburg, as it was detached from the Second Division to guard the approaches to Westminster from Manchester. (usahec)

Emack spread out his troopers on both sides of the road. Tanner's lone cannon, with only a round or two of ammunition remaining, deployed in the middle of the road. At about the same time, Col. Huey's Union brigade, in the rear of Kilpatrick's column, was attacked by Confederate pickets, which were driven back by the 6th Ohio Cavalry. Worried about being hemmed in, Kilpatrick decided to force the issue, mounting a full-scale attack. Two of Custer's regiments thundered up the road and drove the Confederates back, but the attack soon ground to a halt.

The Marylanders did not have long to wait before Custer's 6th Michigan pushed forward on foot, with the 5th Michigan behind it, to drive Emack from the pass, opening a path to the enemy's wagons up ahead. A hill between the Maria Furnace Road and their location blocked any sight of the wagon train, but the men could easily hear the rumbling of the wagons and the bellowing of the livestock. This attack also failed. Tanner's lone cannon fired its last shot, and Emack later wrote how his own "ammunition was entirely exhausted and some of my men actually fought with rocks. . . . they did not give an inch."

Captain Alexander Pennington graduated from West Point on the eve of the Civil War and was assigned to the artillery. He effectively commanded his battery during many campaigns, but like many officers, he switched to the cavalry to achieve faster promotion. (loc)

Kilpatrick brought up two guns from Capt. Alexander Pennington's battery, which opened fire on Emack's Marylanders. Kilpatrick cautioned Pennington from firing into his cavalry, so the artillerist elevated the gun barrels to fire into the passing train and Confederate troopers.

Help for Emack began arriving as soldiers from the 6th Virginia Cavalry and 4th North Carolina Cavalry forced their way through the wagons to the

Brigadier General George Custer's star continued shining as a result of his actions at Monterey Pass. His brigade continued to see action during the remainder of the retreat. (loc)

crest of the pass. According to a soldier in the 6th Virginia Cavalry, "It was with great difficulty that we could get past the wagons in the darkness, and hence our progress was slow, but we finally worked our way up to the front and were dismounted and formed in line as best we could on either side of the road among the rocks and trees. . . ." Some were detailed to advance and attempt to capture Pennington's cannon. A young Virginian recalled that the men would "wait for a lightning flash and then advance a few steps and halt and then [wait] for a light from the batteries and again advance."

The Confederate troopers were steadily pushed back by Custer's dismounted troopers to Red Run and the ridge near the toll house where the Waynesboro-Emmitsburg Turnpike intersected the Maria Furnace Road. However, they were finally halted by Emack's band of tough defenders.

Finally, at about 3:00 a.m., five hours after attempting to push Emack and the defenders from the road, Kilpatrick deployed the 1st West Virginia Cavalry (from Col. Nathaniel Richmond's brigade). The West Virginians were commanded by Capt. Charles Capehart and supported by a company of the 1st Ohio Cavalry. Capehart sent them forward in a vicious saber attack. The almost 700 Union troopers believed they were outnumbered by "five times the[ir] number." According to one Union officer, "a hand-to-hand conflict ensued. The scene was wild and desolating." Captain Emack pulled his sword and rode into the melee. He had already been wounded several times, and was struck three or four times across the shoulder by saber blows. His horse was killed, and Emack was too injured to continue. Some of his men carried him to the rear.

Other Union troopers joined the charge, and flew past the defenders to reach the train, carrying many wounded from the Confederate Second Corps. Capehart earned the Medal of Honor for his actions during the wild action.

Chaos prevailed as Kilpatrick's troopers rode among the wagons. They shot the train's guards and captured scores of wagons. General Jones narrowly avoided capture as Kilpatrick's men closed in. Jones ordered his men to call him "Bill" rather

Brown's Run near the current Monterey Museum saw heavy fighting during the evening of July 4-5 when the 1st West Virginia Cavalry and the 1st Ohio Cavalry drove George Emack's company of Confederate cavalry back toward the Monterey Pass toll house, where many of the wagons were captured. (lg)

than "general," which may have helped him escape. Kilpatrick's troopers probably struck Rodes's trains at the summit of the mountain. The train had stalled because of a disabled wagon up ahead, making it easier for the cavalrymen to capture a section of the train. Many of the wagons were rolled down the side of the mountain, and others were transported with the column toward Maryland.

The Confederates who could still fight retreated down the side of the mountain where Company D of the 1st Maryland Cavalry was stationed. They opened fire on the victorious Union troopers, but were no match for Kilpatrick's overwhelming numbers. Kilpatrick captured hundreds of wagons and over a thousand enemy soldiers. A trooper from the 6th Michigan mused, "It put me in mind of a fourth of July spree to see the wagons all strung along the road, the wheals chopped to pieces, tungs cut off, barrels of liquor smashed in and the wagons set afire."

Kilpatrick realized it was time to retreat when alerted to the approach of Confederate infantry from Alfred Iverson's brigade. The Union troopers quickly finished destroying the wagons and were headed toward Maryland by 7:00 a.m. Kilpatrick estimated his men destroyed seven miles of wagons and captured 1,500 men at a cost of about 100 casualties. One historian estimated a loss of 250 wagons during the attack. Emack was shot through both arms, sustained

Brigadier General Alfred Iverson was an enigma. He effectively commanded his brigade in some battles, but failed horribly at Gettysburg, when he sent his brigade to its destruction near Oak Ridge. He was subsequently banished from the army, but later effectively led a cavalry brigade in Georgia. (loc)

saber cuts to both arms and shoulders, and an artillery projectile hit his right knee, but he survived the ordeal. He sustained surprisingly small losses—one killed and two wounded—but 26 were captured.

Newspaper reporter Edward Paul visited the area after the battle and wrote, "[t]he road is more like the bed of a rocky river, the dirt having been washed away by the heavy rains, left large boulders exposed; where there were not boulders, there was mud and water. . . . Is it to be wondered at that the confederate soldiers unanimously declare that they never will visit Pennsylvania again."

Kilpatrick's Attacks at Fairfield Gap and Leitersburg, Maryland, and the Ride to Smithsburg

As most of Kilpatrick's division headed up South Mountain from the direction of Emmitsburg, he sent most of the 1st Michigan Cavalry, under Lt. Col. Peter Stagg, along Jack's Mountain Road to protect his right flank (the rest of the regiment remained with the column and then rode toward Fairfield Gap to seek out some of the wagons). Stagg's men encountered some of Jones's and Robertson's units guarding the road and an intense fight occurred. The Confederate troopers attacked several times but could not drive Stagg's men away. The Michiganders finally fell back toward the main column but left some companies behind to man a makeshift barricade.

Kilpatrick also sent a portion of the 1st Michigan toward the Fairfield Gap to cut off the wagon train from Fairfield. These men were guided by Hetty Zeilinger, a young 17-year-old girl who lived on a nearby farm. They encountered the 5th North Carolina Cavalry and two companies of the 11th Virginia Cavalry and were forced to return to the main column.

While most of Kilpatrick's men were attacking part of Lee's wagons at Monterey Gap, the 1st Vermont Cavalry had been spun off earlier, and sent into Maryland to seek additional wagons. When asked about the probable route of the wagons, C. H. Buhrman predicted Smithsburg or Leitersburg and agreed to guide the Vermont boys along the mountain roads to these locations. The Green Mountain boys did not find any wagons at Smithsburg, so they headed to Leitersburg. A trooper recalled how "[t]he night was pitch dark, the rain fell in torrents, and the road was rough: a mere wood road over and amongst the rocks." Several horses lost their shoes and became lame. Outside of Leitersburg, they struck gold. Some Confederate cavalry guarded the wagon train, but they were chased off as the Vermonters descended on the wagons, many carrying wounded soldiers. Many Union troopers never forgot the sights and sounds, as some teamsters abandoned their wagons; others were shot, and the mules of many of the driverless wagons headed to their destruction in ravines. The Union cavalry carefully removed the wounded from the wagons and placed them by the side of the road. They destroyed the wagons, and about 100 uninjured Confederates were captured.

Rarely did a cavalry commander experience such a decisive victory. Buhrman, who helped guide both expeditions, estimated Kilpatrick's men destroyed nine miles of wagons (six miles at Monterey Pass and three miles at Leitersburg). The Confederates were justifiably mortified by the magnitude of their losses. Lee and Stuart knew the Union cavalry could be a problem but were uncertain of their potential for destruction. A distraught William Jones offered his resignation to his commander, Jeb Stuart, who did not accept it. Kilpatrick and his men were jubilant. Kilpatrick needed the victory to salve his spirit after his poor performance at Gettysburg. His achievements at Monterey Pass and Leitersburg were particularly remarkable, given the dark night, intense rain, and horrific terrain.

From First Manassas to his death at Yellow Tavern in 1864, Jeb Stuart led the Confederate army's cavalry arm. Dashing and fearless, he was sometimes rash, to the detriment of the army. (loc)

Flush with victory, Kilpatrick continued his ride along the western edge of South Mountain to Ringgold. A cavalryman recalled, "as far as the eye could reach, both front and rear, was a moving mass of horses with motionless riders all wrapped in slumber." All were wet, muddy, and exhausted. The men reached the Maryland town at daybreak and were given a well-deserved two-hour rest. While there, they burned the captured wagons, but not before removing anything of value, such as food, jewelry, and underclothing. The men, including the officers, luxuriated by lying sound asleep in the mud. Soon, the troopers were back in the saddle and heading for Smithsburg under a brightly shining sun. They reached their destination at 9:00 a.m., greeted by grateful civilians lining the streets. Young women sang patriotic songs and showered the men with flowers and fresh bread smeared with jelly and butter. Kilpatrick's band struck up "Hail Columbia" followed by the "Star-Spangled Banner," as some civilians wept in gratitude. Newspaperman Edward Paul noted, "The kind reception met with here did the command more good than a week's rest. Even the horses—faithful animals—seemed to be revived by the patriotic demonstration." Noting the condition of his men, Kilpatrick decided to allow them to rest until the end of the day.

The wagons of Harman's reserve train that escaped Kilpatrick's attacks at Monterrey Pass and Leitersburg began rolling into Hagerstown during the evening of July 5. They were on the road for more than 42 hours and still had hours before reaching Williamsport.

Stuart Catches Up with Kilpatrick at Smithsburg

This woodcut by Allen Christian Redwood dramatically captures the essence of the wagon train of misery. Note the soldiers on the right who were able to walk beside the wagons. (nypl)

Lee's cavalry commander, Jeb Stuart, directly oversaw the activities of a diminished division. Two of his brigades, Fitz Lee's and Hampton's, were away guarding Imboden's wagon train, and two others, Jones's and Robertson's were guarding the roads out of Gettysburg. Stuart retained only Brig. Gen. Rooney Lee's brigade (commanded by Col. John Chambliss) and Brig. Gen. Albert Jenkins' brigade (commanded by Col. Milton Ferguson) to protect Lee's Army of Northern Virginia's left flank during the retreat. This small contingent entered Emmitsburg, Maryland, about dawn on July 5, where Stuart learned a large body of enemy cavalry (Kilpatrick's division)—the civilians estimated it to be 15,000, but Stuart knew they were exaggerating—had passed through the town the day before, heading toward Monterey Pass.

After collecting supplies in Emmitsburg and allowing his men to rest, Stuart struck out toward Cavetown, Maryland, just south of Smithsburg. The men continued securing supplies as they rode south. Stuart's men sorely needed horses and rounded up scores of them. In one instance, a gristmill owner ran out, begging the troopers not to take his horses as they were needed for his operation. He was told they were sorry, but they needed them to get to the Potomac River. If they could cross, the horses would be returned, and they were true to their word. Stuart's men also captured 60-70 prisoners and a wagon train with medical supplies bound for Meade's army.

To get to Cavetown, Stuart's men first crossed the Catoctin Mountains. The road then forked at Deerfield Station, so Stuart broke his command in two "in order to make the passage more certain," sending Chambliss' brigade along the north fork and Ferguson's to the left. Chambliss rode through Raven Rock, which contained "a ravine, having either side precipitous bluffs and spurs." The passageway was defended, forcing Chambliss to dismount most of his men to fight "from crag to crag" to drive the Federals from their path.

Stuart guessed correctly, finding Kilpatrick in Smithsburg. Kilpatrick predicted Stuart would approach from the east, so he deployed his three brigades, each with a battery, on a separate hill north and east of town. He also threw out a picket line to impede Stuart's progress. The Union horse artillery opened fire as Stuart's troopers appeared around 5:00 p.m. For a while, they were the only guns firing, as the Confederate cannon, running low on ammunition, had to be hauled up Nicodemus Hill before they could come into action. After surveying the Union position, Stuart believed he could attack Kilpatrick's left flank, so he ordered Ferguson to come up and join Chambliss. However, instead of riding overland to reach Chambliss, Ferguson pulled his command back to gain the same road Chambliss had taken, using valuable time in the fading daylight.

Kilpatrick observed Ferguson withdrawing and misinterpreted it, thinking Stuart was giving up. With the threat removed, Kilpatrick decided to abandon Smithsburg and head for Boonsboro, which his men reached at 10:00 p.m. July 5 was a long and eventful day for Kilpatrick's cavalry. They had battled at Monterey Pass, captured or destroyed hundreds of Confederate wagons, ridden to Smithsburg, engaged Stuart's Confederate cavalry, and settled in for the night at Boonsboro. In all, they had traveled over 23 miles, and the men and horses were exhausted.

The Smithsburg residents, so filled with glee with the entry of Kilpatrick's troopers earlier in the morning, now sullenly watched Stuart's victorious men riding through the town. Stuart continued to Leitersburg, reuniting with Jones's and Robertson's brigades. Stuart now had a force of four cavalry brigades to screen and protect Lee's army as it continued west toward Williamsport.

Imboden Continues
Toiling Toward Williamsport

It took 13 hours for all of Imboden's wagons to begin the journey to Williamsport from the area around Cashtown. The macadamized Chambersburg Pike proved a mixed blessing. While it provided a stable road surface, it was tough on ill-made and worn shoes, and many army-issued boots fell apart during the journey. Men were so tired they slept "without knowing it … the whole of the army was dozing while marching and moved as if under enchantment or spell—were asleep and at the same time walking." The route bypassed Chambersburg, as the column departed the turnpike, turning left onto Pine Stump Road, considered one of the oldest routes in Franklin County. The narrow road soon became rutted, and mud swallowed feet up to the ankles. A resident noted the column passed his house for 48 hours.

The line of wagons passed through New Franklin and then headed for Marion, Pennsylvania, on its way to Greencastle. However, in the early hours of July 5, a section of train, containing fewer than a dozen wagons, got lost near Marion. The teamster in the lead wagon asked a local citizen for directions to Greencastle. "Take a right at the next road," he was informed, but he was being directed toward Chambersburg. This was a stroke of luck for the wounded, as the Chambersburg citizens provided food and medical assistance until

Union troops arrived to take charge of wounded Confederate soldiers. Jacob Hoke described them as "filthy, bloody, with wounds undressed and swarming with vermin, and almost famished for food and water, they presented such a sight as I hope I may never see again."

John Imboden's wagons filled with wounded soldiers made fairly good time while on Chambersburg Pike's macadam surface. His problems began when the wagons turned onto side roads. (achs)

Wagons breaking down, or becoming so mired in mud they could not be extricated, lay scattered along the train's route, as did all manner of knapsacks, blankets, clothing, and supplies. Many residents responded to knocks on their doors, finding the walking wounded Confederate soldiers begging for food and medical attention. Confederates regularly fanned out to visit farms to confiscate wagons that could be used to replace those worn out or hopelessly stuck in the mud. Henry Hege later wrote a relative, "they took everything they could make use of … Some of the rebels appear to be nice clever men. Some of them would harm no man or steal anything. But I tell you the greatest portion of them are nothing but thieves and robbers and some murder[er]s."

The trip became increasingly hard on the wounded. Hege recalled a chorus of groans and shrieks every time a wagon hit a bump. Rev. J. C. Smith explained how those with wounds to their lower extremities and those with more serious ones rode in wagons; those with upper body wounds or less serious ones limped alongside the wagons.

Daybreak of July 5 brought the van of Imboden's wagons into Greencastle, Pennsylvania. The Maryland line loomed just ahead—a mere 12-15 miles to the train's Williamsport destination. Imboden recalled: "[h]ere our apprehended troubles began." After the 18th Virginia Cavalry passed through town at the head of the column and had progressed almost a mile beyond town, about three dozen townspeople descended upon an undefended portion of the train, hacking at the wheels of 10-12 wagons with axes, causing the vehicles to fall to the ground with a thump that caused further misery to the wounded within. Townspeople were angry over a Confederate raiding party that ransacked Greencastle earlier in the

The son of Adm. John Dahlgren, Capt. Ulric Dahlgren was not satisfied with his role as a staff officer and led troops in combat whenever he could. After recovering from the amputation of his leg at the battle of Hagerstown, Dahlgren helped lead a cavalry expedition against Richmond in February 1864, but it cost him his life. (loc)

campaign, and sought their revenge. A detachment of Virginians galloped back to town and halted the destruction. Imboden told his men to capture the civilians and treat them as prisoners of war.

This was just the beginning, for Imboden recalled, "Union cavalry began to swarm down upon us from fields and cross roads, making their attacks in small bodies, and striking the column when there were few or no guards and thus creating great confusion." One attack by about 100 troopers from the 6th Pennsylvania Cavalry under Capt. Ulric Dahlgren was accompanied by a couple dozen Greencastle citizens. Attacking Unionists captured more than 130 wagons and 200 prisoners (most of them wounded), and 300 horses and mules. However, Confederate cavalry arrived, driving away the Pennsylvanians, freeing several wagons and prisoners. Civilians grabbed cows and horses and ran away with them.

The train experienced several more hit-and-run attacks as it continued south. General Imboden was almost captured during one melee. A major attack occurred at about the middle of the wagon train as it approached Cunningham's Crossroads (now Cearfoss), a few miles inside of Maryland, and midway between Greencastle and Williamsport. Around 200 troopers from the 1st New York Cavalry and 12th Pennsylvania Cavalry, under the command of Capt. Abram Jones, descended on the train, capturing over 100 wagons, about 650 prisoners, more than 300 horses and mules, and two cannon. Confederate horsemen counterattacked, but were not strong enough to recapture the wagons, which Union cavalry quickly whisked away.

While Union cavalry attacked the van and middle section of Imboden's wagons, Col. Irvin Gregg's brigade (Gen. David Gregg's division) confronted the train's rear near Caledonia Furnace, about seven miles from Cashtown. Riding along Chambersburg Pike, these troopers had already captured 2,000 stragglers and 2,800 wounded enemy soldiers along the way from Cashtown. Brigadier General Fitz Lee's Confederate cavalry brigade guarded the rear wagons, and drove the Union troopers away. The gray-clad troopers continued marching toward Greencastle, closely followed by Gregg's cavalry.

It is unclear where this scene, entitled "Wounded Confederate Getting Help," occurred, but it could easily have been when some wayward Confederate wagons entered Chambersburg, Pennsylvania, allowing the wounded to receive the medical assistance they desperately needed. (loc)

The first of Imboden's wagons rolled into Williamsport during the afternoon of July 5. Imboden received a scare when he learned of a sizeable Union force holding the town, but the report was unfounded. The wagon train now stretched over 30 miles, so it would take a considerable time to reach safety. Imboden expected the wagons to immediately cross the Potomac River on the pontoon bridge Lee left there, or so Imboden thought. The bridge was built on June 15 to span the river at Falling Waters, about four miles south of Williamsport. As the army marched north toward Pennsylvania, the bridge was left in place, guarded only by a small complement of teamsters, infantrymen, and engineers. Although important to Lee, no one thought to secure it with an adequate defensive force. A small Union cavalry force of about 300 men from four regiments, under the command of Maj. Shadrock Foley of the 14th Pennsylvania Cavalry, headed toward the Potomac to secure or destroy the bridge. The detachment pounced on the morning of July 4, driving away its defenders and burning or destroying the pontoons. Unbeknownst to Imboden, his path across the Potomac River was gone. He learned of the catastrophe when he arrived at Williamsport. Meade did not discover this critical development until 7:00 p.m. on July 5.

Oddly, Imboden never mentioned the loss of the pontoon bridge in his post-war writings, only mentioning how the heavy rains swelling the Potomac River had eliminated the possibility of fording it. The river was over five feet deep and rising, while swift currents carried logs and other debris downstream. Only a small ferry boat plied the river, which Harman

used to send perishable goods across to Virginia,
two wagons at a time. Imboden decided to convert
Williamsport into a "great hospital" for thousands
of wounded. "The town was taken possession of,"
he wrote after the war, and "all of the churches,
schoolhouses, etc. were converted into hospitals, and
proving insufficient, many of the private houses were
occupied." He created a large park to house wagons
along the C&O Canal basin and waited.

Although the first of Imboden's wagons finally
rolled into Williamsport, it took 16 hours for the last
wagon to arrive. Another major issue faced Imboden:
Gen. John Buford's First Cavalry Division was heading
in his direction with orders to attack Williamsport,
destroy wagons, and capture the wounded. Buford's
men, who played a major role in the first day's fighting
at Gettysburg, left Adams County on July 2 and
arrived at Westminster, Maryland, on July 3 to refit
and guard the army's trains. Upon learning of Lee's
movement, Buford put his men back in the saddle
by noon on July 4, riding 25 miles toward Frederick.
He aimed his men toward Williamsport, which he
thought to be the crossing point of the Confederates.
While his men were bivouacking on the evening of
July 4-5, Buford identified a camp visitor as a spy and
ordered him hanged. The body dangled for days as
a lesson to anyone thinking of following in the spy's
footsteps. The exhausted troopers entered Frederick
at 7:00 p.m. on July 5, where they resupplied and
spent the night. When Gen. William French learned
of Confederate wagons rolling through Hagerstown
on their way to Williamsport, he informed Buford the
time was right for an attack.

Lee Continues His Retreat

Ambrose Wright's men finally reached the top of Monterey Pass at daybreak on July 5. It took them six hours to travel six miles and reach the top of the mountain on a crowded road heavily rutted by wagon tracks. According to Gen. Wright, "I came upon the rear of the train upon the top of the mountain, but found the road so completely blocked up as to prevent my farther progress. I halted my command, and permitted the men to lie down and take a little rest, while I rode to the front, to ascertain the exact condition of affairs." The men threw themselves to the ground and quickly fell asleep in the driving rain. Although ready to provide support, they learned the danger to the wagons had already passed. Wright conferred with Gen. Iverson, and the two brigades marched down the side of the mountain toward Waynesboro.

The men of Anderson's division (A. P. Hill's Corps) were strung out between Fairfield and Monterey Pass during the morning of July 5, with Dorsey Pender's and Harry Heth's divisions behind them near Fairfield. The men of Longstreet's First Corps were told to leave the battlefield and follow Hill's Corps to Fairfield. They were to be ready to march by sundown on July 4, which changed to 10:00 a.m. The march did not begin until the early morning hours of July 5. It took 12 hours for Hill's Corps to clear the road before Longstreet's men could take up the march.

Second Corps commander Lt. Gen. Richard Ewell probably had the most to fret about as his corps formed the rearguard out of Gettysburg. He noted in his report by "10:00 a.m. on the 5th, the other corps were not all in the road, and, consequently, mine did not take up its march till near noon, and only reached Fairfield at 4 p.m." As Ewell's men finally pulled onto the road, a glance behind them showed burning embers of at least a dozen homes on the western edge of Gettysburg that were set ablaze, lest Union sharpshooters occupy them to wreak havoc on Ewell's men. Lee timed Ewell's withdrawal from Seminary Ridge to coincide with Longstreet's Corps' march toward Fairfield Road. Ewell's men halted near Willoughby Run, three miles west of Gettysburg, to allow Longstreet's men to continue their march west on

Lieutenant General Richard Ewell, or "Old Bald Head," assumed command of the Confederate Second Corps after Stonewall Jackson's death at Chancellorsville. An aggressive fighter up to the loss of his leg at Second Manassas, Ewell was less effective as a corps commander, and Lee removed him from command during the summer of 1864. (loc)

Dependable and valued by Lee, Lt. Gen. James Longstreet commanded the Confederate First Corps until he was severely wounded during the Overland Campaign in early May 1864. (loc)

Fairfield Road. Such an approach ensured both corps were within supporting distance, if the need arose.

It took Lee's infantry about 18 hours to finally get onto Fairfield Road, and as the last unit joined the march, the retreating army's column stretched almost to the Potomac River. Reserve wagons and Ewell's trains led the column, and were closest to Williamsport. The troops and their wagons and ambulances came next. Almost 4,000 prisoners, guarded by Pickett's division, were tucked behind Hood's division. Prisoners were organized into divisions, marching four men abreast on Fairfield Road, with guards marching along both sides of the road. Officers were separated from enlisted men, marching in single file.

Lee's journey to Hagerstown on July 5 was painstakingly slow, about a mile an hour. Division commander General Robert Rodes called it a "most wearisome march in mud and rain." Exhausted men had little to eat, and when there was a break, men slunk to the ground, actually mud, and fell sound asleep.

Most of Lee's army was a sorry sight. Private William Fletcher of the 5th Texas recalled, "My shoes were old and so were my clothes. . . . My pants were frazzled and split up to the knees so I cut them off just below the knees . . . no socks or drawers. . . . It was not long after leaving camp, marching in mud about six inches deep I lost the sole of one shoe. . . ." He finally pulled off both shoes and attempted to make his way home barefooted.

General James Longstreet realized the vulnerability of the column and whenever they halted, he "walked ceaselessly backward and forward like a sailor on his quarterdeck," recalled one staff officer. He reported, "Our march was much impeded by heavy rains and excessively bad roads. We succeeded, however, in reaching the top of the mountain early in the night of the 5th."

Lee lost thousands of men in the days immediately after the battle when Union cavalry attacked his trains. He explained another source of losses in a communication to President Jefferson Davis: "The day after the last battle at Gettysburg, on sending back the train with the wounded, it was reported that about 5,000 well men started back at night to overtake it.

I fear most of these were captured by the enemy's cavalry and armed citizens, who beset their route."

Meade Waits to Determine Lee's Actions

Because Meade unleashed his cavalry against Lee's wagons, he could not use them to defend his supply route from Westminster, through Littlestown and Two Taverns. Instead of the horse soldiers, he sent the II and XII Corps infantrymen. He also worried about his vulnerable left flank, so he sent the V Corps toward Marsh Creek. He could call on other troops, should the need arise.

Major General John Sedgwick rose through the ranks to become commander of the Union VI Corps during the Gettysburg Campaign. Beloved by his men, he was killed by a sniper during the battle of Spotsylvania. (loc)

Meade knew at least part of Lee's army was in motion on July 4, but was unsure of its locations and intentions. Meade decided to use his least used and freshest unit, Maj. Gen. John Sedgwick's VI Corps, to advance through fields toward Fairfield Road at 12:30 p.m. on July 5. Meade provided clear orders: "Push forward your column in a westerly direction. Fire on his force. If rear guard, it will be compelled to return; if not, you will find out." Meade then informed Sedgwick of the importance of his mission: "Time is of great importance, as I cannot give orders for a movement without explicit information from you."

The march across the battlefield to reach Fairfield Road tried Sedgwick's troops. "Dead men, dead horses, guns, equipment, caissons, shot and shell and all the paraphernalia and appurtenances of the battlefield scattered and shattered in in painful profusion . . . . Every barn on the line of march was filled to overflowing with the rebel wounded, the dying and the dead," according to one of the soldiers.

Although Maj. Gen. William French played a minor role during the Gettysburg Campaign, he saw extensive action as a brigade and division commander earlier in the war. After Gettysburg, he assumed command of the Union III Corps. (loc)

While awaiting additional intelligence about Lee's army, Meade penned a message to General in Chief Henry Halleck at 8:30 a.m., informing him "the enemy retired, under cover of the night and heavy rain, in the direction of Fairfield and Cashtown" and Union cavalry was in hot pursuit on the enemy's left and rear. He promised to move "at once on his [Lee's] flank, via Middletown and South Mountain Pass." He also told Halleck that his army's strength had shrunk to about 55,000 effectives, exclusive of cavalry, and requested "[e]very available re-enforcement is required, and should be sent to Frederick without delay." Halleck

Although Maj. Gen. Jubal Early only commanded a division during the Gettysburg Campaign, he often played a disproportionate role in Lee's planning. He rose to command the Confederate Second Corps that invaded Maryland during the summer of 1864. (loc)

approved Meade's planned movements as "perfectly satisfactory," and his call for reinforcements "has been anticipated." Halleck intended to put all of Couch's inexperienced troops at his disposal. He told Meade he could count on Maj. Gen. William French's troops as well.

A signal station on Little Round Top sent corroboration of Lee's retreat at 8:40 a.m.: "Can see what appears to be quite a heavy body of troops halted on the road leading from Chambersburg pike toward the Fairfield road, northwest from this point. . . . The troops of Ewell seen on the right from this point yesterday have disappeared." Another message arrived at headquarters ten minutes later: "The enemy's column, reported halted, is now moving to the left, toward the Fairfield road."

While Meade continued collecting information on Lee's whereabouts and intentions, he met with Brig. Gen. Herman Haupt, charged with repairing the railroads in the area. An old friend of Meade's, Haupt asked the army commander about his plans and received the disheartening news that Meade contemplated a cautious pursuit of Lee. Meade expressed concerns about the lack of supplies and horses, as well as the condition of his men. A discouraged Haupt immediately left for Washington to discuss the matter directly with Halleck, hoping that the General-in-Chief could light a fire under Meade. Historian Kent Masterson Brown faulted Haupt for possibly poisoning Meade's relationship with Lincoln and Halleck, particularly since the railroader lacked the necessary background information to make an informed judgment.

The Fight at Granite Hill

As Meade and Haupt chatted, Sedgwick's corps continued their reconnaissance to determine the position of Lee's army. Brigadier General Horatio Wright's division led the column. A report of Rebel troops in front of the marchers caused Sedgwick's men to halt and throw up rudimentary breastworks. It was a false alarm, and the line again moved toward Fairfield Road. Men gripped their muskets, ready for a fight, although they only encountered stragglers on the road. Because the mud and driving rain turned the road into mush, they had only marched about six miles along Fairfield Road by 6:00 p.m. A couple of miles outside Fairfield, men could see a long line of wagons moving through town with a strong Confederate line of defense in front of them.

Sedgwick was itching for a fight as his men had not shared in the glory at Gettysburg. He sought to bring his ordnance trains with him to ensure an adequate supply of ammunition. Meade denied the request, as this was merely a reconnaissance to "ascertain the position and movement" of the enemy. Brigadier General Gouverneur Warren, Meade's chief engineer, accompanied Sedgwick. The corps received orders to return to its original position as soon as possible and be ready for a general movement in pursuit of Lee. Colonel John McIntosh's cavalry brigade screened the movement. Why Meade sent a full infantry corps on a reconnaissance with no intention for combat is unclear. The almost 20-mile round-trip reconnaissance mission took its toll on the men, making it difficult for the VI Corps to move quickly after Lee's army in the future.

Brigadier General Horatio Wright had seen limited action when he was given command of a division in the Union VI Corps. He assumed command of the corps upon Sedgwick's death. (loc)

The van of the VI Corps had finally encountered Lee's rearguard, composed of Maj. Gen. Jubal Early's division of Ewell's Second Corps. General Early's division's baggage train had bogged down in the mud in Fairfield, stalling his troop's movements, and leaving him vulnerable to attack. Early sent messengers to hurry the wagons along, without any luck. Finally, in frustration, he ordered Col. Hilary Jones's Artillery Battalion to unlimber and fire blank charges toward the wagons. This did the trick, as horses quickly extracted themselves from the muck and continued on their way toward the foot of South Mountain.

Lieutenant Colonel Elijah White and his 35th Virginia Cavalry Battalion closely watched Sedgwick's men crest a rise called "Granite Hill," and quickly sent a courier with the news to Early. He realized the threat and the need to hold the enemy in check. Early marched back Brig. Gen. John Gordon's Georgia infantry brigade to delay the enemy's pursuit. The Virginians and Georgians were joined by the Louisiana Guard Artillery.

General Wright deployed his division in a line across Fairfield Road, stretching out half a mile from flank to flank, and sent skirmishers toward the enemy. The corps' other two divisions were ready for action in the rear, should they be needed. Wright also brought up Col. Charles Tompkins's artillery brigade. The two sides exchanged artillery fire, but the Union's advantage in firepower was soon evident. Private Wilbur Fisk of the 2nd Vermont explained just before reaching Fairfield, "we met a couple of rebel shells that informed us that our further progress was disputed very decidedly. Our batteries sent back shells enough to pay them and leave the heavy balance in our favor."

Gordon sprung his 26th Georgia Infantry on a sudden bayonet charge that scattered the Union skirmish line, sending it back toward the main line. The heroic charge did what was intended—delay Sedgwick's advance to give wagons and Early's infantry time to leave Fairfield.

One of the several hills between Gettysburg and Fairfield, Granite Hill, and the Union troops scaling it, could be seen by the Confederates further west during the early phases of the post-Gettysburg Campaign. (lg)

The skirmish at Granite Hill lasted only about an hour, as nightfall ended the action. Meade's orders not to engage in a serious fight dictated Sedgwick's cautious approach. There were few casualties during this skirmish, despite Tompkins's guns firing more than 160 shells. The 26th Georgia lost two men killed and eleven wounded; Wright lost one killed and two wounded.

Following Meade's orders, Sedgwick could not aggressively push Gordon's men. Instead, he gingerly followed the retreating Rebels. He was already eight miles from the rest of the army and in a potentially vulnerable situation. One VI Corps division commander, Brig. Gen. Albion Howe, later testified, "we waited for them [Early's men] to go on. There seemed to be no disposition to push this rearguard when we got up to Fairfield."

Ewell summed up the action by stating in his report: "Here the enemy, who had been threatening our rear and occasionally opening a fire of artillery on the rear guard, showed more boldness in attacking, throwing out a line of skirmishers over a mile in length. They were repulsed, and a battery which was shelling our column driven off." His report was fairly accurate, except for his last statement. Sedgwick also gave a fairly accurate account of the fight, adding his corps captured 250 prisoners during its excursion.

Sedgwick followed his orders: not to bring on an engagement but to gather the information Meade needed to decide his next moves. The VI Corps commander reported Lee's rearguard had reached Fairfield, and the entire column was moving through South Mountain. He could not know Lee had no intention of staging a rearguard fight in the mountains.

Meade and Sedgwick were criticized for not pressing the rear of Lee's army more vigorously. A soldier in the 93rd Pennsylvania complained, they had "scarcely pressed them at all, as far as I could judge," and a member of the 5th Maine wrote, "We came up to their rear . . . and gave them a few shell and shot to hurry them." Many retreating Confederates were clearly worried about a full-scale attack. A member of the 5th Alabama explained how the "troops & wagons [were] crowded together in the little valley. . . . I was somewhat uneasy that the enemy might do us some damage." Major General Abner Doubleday, no fan of Meade after being removed from temporary command of the Union I Corps after the first day of the battle, felt the army missed a great opportunity to attack Lee's rear while the Union cavalry hit the wagon trains.

Division commander Brig. Gen. Albion Howe did not see action during the battle of Gettysburg but was an active participant in the army's pursuit. His abrasive behavior led to his removal from command during the latter part of 1863. (loc)

Lee Splits His Army as Meade Plans His Pursuit

Lee split the column as it left Fairfield because he worried that Meade's infantry would aggressively pursue his army. Hill's Third Corps (marching in front of the army) continued along Maria Furnace Road toward Monterey Pass; Longstreet's First Corps followed Jack's Mountain Road, east of the Maria Furnace Road. Both roads emptied into the Emmitsburg-Waynesboro Turnpike, but Longstreet's path brought him further south of the Monterey Pass. Longstreet's march up the mountainside corresponded to Kilpatrick's route during the evening of July 4-5. Men of Hood's division led the corps, the van reaching Monterey Pass at 1:00 a.m. on July 6, where they bivouacked for the night. McLaws's division remained near the mountain's base, and Pickett's division guarding the prisoners was in-between the two divisions when the march halted for the night. Exhausted men were ordered to quickly assemble defensive works, facing east. Hill's Corps guarded the western face of the mountain, also throwing up breastworks. As Ewell's men began leaving Fairfield, Lee directed them along Maria Furnace Road, by now clear of troops and wagons but a muddy quagmire.

Thousands of Union prisoners in the middle of Longstreet's column were in bad shape. They were hungry and without supplies, and suffered the emotional trauma of being captured and their unknown fate. One of Longstreet's aides, Maj. John Fairfax, seeing prisoners' anguish, took it upon himself to begin paroling them, until Lee himself ordered him to stop.

Lee rode along with the rearguard. He "halted our corps and told General Ewell to try to induce the enemy to fight. . . . If 'those people' will only come out and give us an open field fight, we will smash them," according to Isaac Seymour, the adjutant general of Hays's brigade (Early's division). Seymour served through the war, but "never saw General Lee so anxious for a fight." Lee did not know Sedgwick had been ordered to follow him, and had no knowledge of Sedgwick's orders to avoid an engagement.

With Lee's retreat no longer in doubt, Meade plotted his pursuit. He decided on Middletown, Maryland, as his assembly point. The army would move along the eastern side of South Mountain, following a parallel track to Lee's army. Moving seven infantry corps, artillery, and wagons over a restricted road system, which had turned to mud during the rainy downpours, proved difficult. Meade worked closely with his staff and engineers to craft routes for each corps, but he did not wish to disseminate the plans until he received Sedgwick's report.

By the evening of July 5, Meade felt he had enough information on Lee's movements and intentions, so he released the marching orders for the army to recombine at Middletown. The I, III, and VI, under Sedgwick (right wing), would march to Emmitsburg and then to Mechanicstown, Lewistown, Hamburg, and finally Middletown. The V and XI Corps, under Howard (center wing), would also head over to Emmitsburg, but then head south via Creagerstown, Utica, Highknob Pass, and finally to Middletown. The

II and XII Corps, under Slocum (left wing), would march to Taneytown, Middleburg, Woodsborough, Frederick to Middletown. Trains would remain with their respective corps. The Reserve Artillery would travel from Taneytown to Middletown.

Still, the cautious Meade felt he needed additional information before moving his army. He continued worrying about Lee's intentions when his Confederate troops reached the mountains. Did he intend to fight there? Moving an army involved more than merely pointing troops in a certain direction. It also entailed ensuring they had adequate supplies. As the army moved west, it necessitated a change in the base of supplies from Westminster to Frederick (which contained a major spur of the Baltimore and Ohio Railroad), and Meade did not want to order this difficult procedure until sure of Lee's retreat route and motives. The decision was so critical that Meade hesitated until he had more definitive proof. The uncertainty caused by Lee's slow march delayed the start of Meade's pursuit for nearly 30 hours and gave the Confederate army the space it needed to head west to the Potomac River without the Union army nipping at its heels.

In addition to rescinding marching orders, Meade informed his commanders of his decision to retain his headquarters at Gettysburg, at least for the time being. However, other troops had already left Gettysburg in accordance with Meade's circular before being ordered to halt. The V Corps had marched about 4-5 miles before halting on Emmitsburg Road, and the XI Corps marched down Taneytown Road a short distance from the battlefield.

Both armies expended much of their ammunition during the battle, but Meade expected a faster resupply. Until he received additional stocks, however, Meade ordered: "no ammunition be exhausted unless there is reason to believe that its use will produce a decided effect upon the enemy." The availability of horses continued to plague Meade and his cavalry commander, Alfred Pleasonton. The latter requested 2,000 mounts being held in Washington be sent at once.

CAPTAIN ULRIC DAHLGREN

— ▼ —

Commanded a detachment of Union cavalry that made a surprise attack on a larger force of Confederate cavalry on this square, July 2, 1863. Important papers for General Lee were taken from the men who were captured.

PENNSYLVANIA HISTORICAL AND MUSEUM COMMISSION

Another Day of Cavalry Fights

CHAPTER FOUR
JULY 6, 1863

General Imboden called the situation in Williamsport "frightful." Fording the river was impossible as torrential rains had swelled the depth to 13 feet. A small ferry boat plied the river, but progress was exceedingly slow. Imboden realized this mode of transportation could not transport the 5,000 wagons and ambulances crammed into Williamsport. He immediately ordered the streets barricaded with wagons, and waited.

Lee's battered army spent the night of July 5-6 in and around South Mountain, extending almost 20 miles from Waynesboro to Fairfield. Ewell's Second Corps remained in the rear, camping about a mile and a half west of Fairfield. Ewell's men were to rotate to the front of Lee's column, but the mountains and proximity of the enemy made such a movement impossible. Ewell did rotate his divisions. Early's division, which formed the rearguard during the initial retreat, now formed the van of the corps, followed by Johnson's division, while Rodes's division brought up the rear. Wagons and infantry from other

The marker on the Greencastle, Pennsylvania, town square explains Ulric Dahlgren's exploits while the battle of Gettysburg was raging. He also led a small cavalry detachment into this area after the battle that destroyed and captured some of Lee's retreating wagons. (lg)

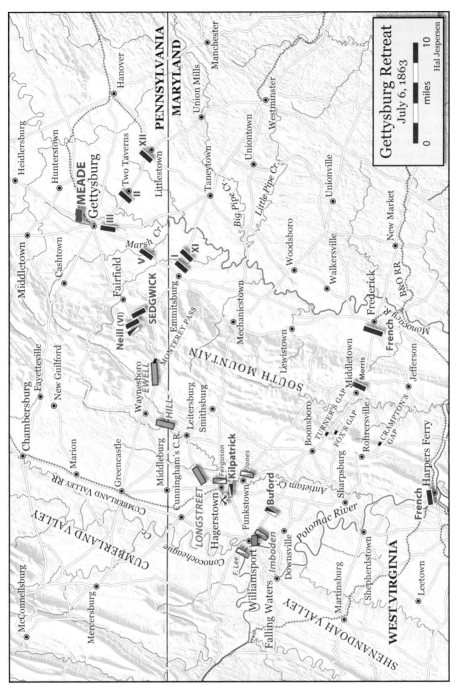

JULY 6—Both armies were on the road, but Lee's head start allowed his First Corps to reach Hagerstown. Meade dispersed his army on different roads as he began his pursuit of the Confederate army. All of Lee's wagons reached Williamsport, only to find the pontoon bridge gone.

The sway of the trees, the soldiers wearing ponchos, and the general gloom illustrate the rainy conditions during the initial march of Meade's army after Lee. (loc)

commands still blocked the road ahead, so Ewell did not leave the Fairfield area to scale the side of South Mountain until the early afternoon of July 6. The men were angered by the sight of remnants of their burned wagons, often pushed to the side of the road. Many contained the fragments of their clothes and other personal belongings.

Up ahead, Lee's other two corps finished their journey over South Mountain on July 6. Lee thought Hill's progress up the mountain was too slow, so the Third Corps was ordered to wait until Longstreet's First Corps marched past it on Emmitsburg-Waynesboro Turnpike. Longstreet rotated his divisions, so McLaws's division led the march, followed by Hood. Longstreet carefully tucked a battalion of artillery behind the brigade in the van. McLaws's three remaining infantry brigades followed with the division's trains, and the remainder of its artillery brought up the rear. Next came three of Hood's brigades, followed by their trains. Hood's fourth brigade formed the corps' rearguard. When the last of Longstreet's men passed, Hill's men gathered their meager possessions and continued marching. Heth's division led the corps, followed by Pender's and then Anderson's divisions. Pickett's division and the 4,000 Union prisoners marched with Hill's corps. Lee also rode with Hill, remaining in the middle of his retreating army. It took Longstreet's and Hill's men nine hours to clear the road before Ewell's troops could get underway. Their march began between 1:00–3:00 p.m.

Free from the mountains, Lee's troops could make swifter progress on the paved roads of the Cumberland

Major General George Pickett will always be associated with the disastrous charge at Gettysburg. After a series of assignments, Pickett returned to command a division in Lee's army, which was soundly thrashed at the decisive battle of Five Forks. (loc)

Valley. Lee was spurred on by the knowledge that his trains, congregating at Williamsport, remained vulnerable and needed protection. After marching through downtown Waynesboro, Longstreet turned left and headed for Leitersburg, Maryland, about five miles away. Hagerstown was another seven miles down the road, but the fast pace allowed the van to reach it by 5:00 p.m. on July 6—not long after the cavalry fight in the streets had ended. This surprised Longstreet, who noted, "[a]s our exhausted men and animals were not in condition for rapid movement, I thought myself fortunate when I found that I could reach Hagerstown in time to relieve our trains at Williamsport, then seriously threatened."

Lee's difficult journey has seldom been duplicated. For example, Longstreet's First Corps did not begin its march from Gettysburg until 1:00 a.m. on July 5 and marched 19 hours, rested for three, and then undertook another 14-hour march to Hagerstown. Jubilant crowds celebrating the Confederate defeat lined the streets. In response to the jeers hurled at the Confederates trudging along the road, an artilleryman observed, "it is true we did not gain a victory [at Gettysburg], but we are far from being defeated. A great part of our want of success is attributed to our falling short of rifle gun ammunition, immense quantities of which were fired by our army." Several officers and visitors confirmed Lee's dire need of ammunition, which was estimated could last only one additional day of battle.

Civilians complained of losing livestock, grains, and hay as Lee's army continued scouring for supplies along the retreat path. The quartermasters of each brigade handled the foraging by detailing one company from each regiment to gather supplies. Foragers usually followed a route parallel to the rest of the troops, scooping up supplies whenever they encountered them. Captain James Wood of Company D, 37th Virginia (Steuart's brigade; Johnson's division; Second Corps) recalled how his men were ordered to detour to gather supplies. "My route was over a mile out and parallel with the course of the column," he wrote. "The well supplied homes enabled me to soon load the wagons and get them underway on the country road that converged toward the column." Officers provided Confederate currency to "purchase"

Many illustrations exist of Confederate prisoners making their way to prisoner of war camps, but none of Union prisoners. Although this illustration shows Confederate prisoners, but for their uniforms, these men could easily be Union prisoners. (loc)

the goods. These foraging details were vulnerable to attacks from Union units following Lee's army—Wood's company fought off such an attack.

Sedgwick Probes Lee's Rear

Dawn of July 6 found the Union VI Corps in position outside of Fairfield. Its commander had already received a message from Meade at 2:00 a.m., to "push your reconnaissance, so as to ascertain, if practicable, how far the enemy has retreated, and also the character of the gap and practicability of carrying the same, in case I should determine to advance on that line."

Sedgwick waited until the sun had risen to see his surroundings. He told Meade he was "afraid to move my whole command, on account of the character of the country and density of the fog." He could not determine whether Lee had taken the road to Hagerstown or Emmitsburg, but civilians told him the enemy was moving in both directions. Sedgwick decided to send Brig. Gen. Thomas Neill's brigade (Brig. Gen. Albion Howe's division), screened by Col. John McIntosh's cavalry brigade, forward to determine the enemy's strength. He believed, "from the immense number of camp-fires seen last evening that the enemy have a very strong rear guard, and will hold the gaps strongly." The skirmish line did not

John McIntosh was considered to be one of the most effective Union cavalry commanders. Wounded several times during the war, his right leg was amputated after the battle of Third Winchester in 1864. He quickly recuperated and returned to his command. (usahec)

initially encounter enemy soldiers, so Sedgwick continued Neill's movement until it encountered Gen. Rodes' rearguard, composed of Brig. Gen. Daniel's brigade.

Brigade commander Junius Daniel turned his 45th North Carolina back to face Neill's men. Some of the Tar Heels occupied a wheat field on a knoll west of

This woodcut shows the march of the VI Corps after Lee's army on Fairfield Road. Note the town of Fairfield in the background. (loc)

Fairfield. The North Carolinians were ordered to fix bayonets and charge, driving the Union soldiers before them. Rodes brought up Brig. Gen. George Doles' brigade to help discourage any determined Union push against the rearguard. A New Jersey soldier said they "found the enemy in such force in the gap that [we] were nearly all day in dislodging him." Sedgwick

A Virginian by birth, Brig. Gen. John Newton commanded a division in the Union VI Corps during the early stages of the Gettysburg Campaign. Upon John Reynolds's death on July 1, Newton was tapped to command the Union I Corps. When the corps was dissolved, Newton assumed command of a division in William Sherman's army. (loc)

Meade's army pursues Lee in this Edwin Forbes drawing. (loc)

realized the enemy held the advantage at the gap and he decided not to push forward.

Meade responded again to Sedgwick at 9:00 a.m. to reassure his isolated infantry corps commander "evidence seems to show a[n enemy] movement to Hagerstown and the Potomac. No doubt the principal force is between Fairfield and Hagerstown; but I apprehend they will be likely to let you alone, if you let them alone." Meade wanted to know more about Neill's cautious pursuit and told Sedgwick, "[w]henever I am satisfied that the main body [of the enemy] is retiring from the mountains, I shall continue my flank movement."

Confusing messages from headquarters and wing commanders filled the morning of July 6. Major General John Newton, now commanding the I Corps, wanted to move south, but was told at 2:00 a.m.: "The commanding general does not wish to have your command move, unless you receive orders to do so from General Sedgwick." An hour later, he informed Meade's headquarters that Sedgwick had permitted him to proceed to Emmitsburg with the III Corps, and intended to begin the movement at 5:00 a.m. The march put two depleted units within supporting distance of the VI Corps. However, a staff officer galloped up to Newton with a message from headquarters, drafted at 7:40 a.m.: "It appears from a dispatch just received from General Sedgwick that he had given no orders for the movement of your command, and while the commanding general does not at this moment attach any blame to any one for the misapprehension of instructions which has led to your movement this morning, he considers it unfortunate that the orders of General Sedgwick were not given in writing."

Meade halted the I and III Corps' movements, as Sedgwick apparently did not coordinate them. The army commander then brought up additional troops within supporting distance of Sedgwick. He ordered Oliver Howard, overseeing movements of his own XI Corps and the V Corps, to send one of them to Emmitsburg (about 10 miles from Gettysburg) and the other to Fairfield. Sedgwick could rely on support from four other infantry corps, comprising more than 70% of Meade's army. Meade's other two corps were south of Gettysburg. The II Corps spent the day at Two Taverns (about five miles from Gettysburg), and the XII Corps was in Littlestown (10 miles from Gettysburg).

Meade was concerned by a report from Sedgwick suggesting "a large force of the enemy in the mountains." The army commander responded by writing to Halleck at 2:00 p.m. that he "deemed it prudent to suspend the movement to Middletown until I could be certain the enemy were evacuating the Cumberland Valley." Although Meade admitted the difficulty in getting reliable information, he finally ascertained that the "enemy is retreating, very much crippled, and hampered with his trains." Meade ended the communication by continuing to echo his concerns: "I shall not move the army from its present position until I am better satisfied the enemy are evacuating the Cumberland Valley."

Although a Georgian by birth, Brig. Gen. Montgomery Meigs opposed secession and remained with the Union. He occupied the critically important position of quartermaster general of the U.S. Army, providing all manner of needed supplies to the troops. He was known as an efficient, hard-driving, and scrupulously honest officer. (loc)

Meade Decides Next Steps

Although his army was not entirely in motion, Meade worked tirelessly on the necessary logistics for a pursuit. Several officers were tasked with addressing the army's need for additional horses. Henry Haupt wrote to the presidents of several railroads in the area that "[e]xtraordinary efforts should be made by the officers of all railroads over which horses are transported to push them forward without delay, day and night. Please give this subject prompt personal attention." Quartermaster General M. C. Meigs reported 1,600 horses left Frederick by midday on July 6, and hundreds of other horses were being collected. He promised another 5,000 were on their way from all around the Union. To feed the massive numbers of livestock, the department sent 750,000 pounds of grain and 250,000 pounds of hay each day to Frederick and then onto Meade's army.

Halleck also made thousands of reinforcements available. Major General Robert Schenck, who commanded the Middle Department headquartered in Baltimore, rounded up about 18,000 men from his

Major General Robert Schenck saw extensive action during the Civil War until a wound at the battle of Second Bull Run permanently damaged his right arm. He was assigned command of the VIII Corps during the Gettysburg Campaign, tasked with protecting the vital Baltimore and Ohio Railroad. (loc)

various commands and sent them northward. Some of these troops were veterans; others were inexperienced. An additional 6,000 men under Brig. Gen. Benjamin Kelley were marching from Cumberland, Maryland, to join Meade. All these troops were on top of thousands Darius Couch sent from his Department of the Susquehanna. However, some rookies saw financial opportunities, causing the department's assistant adjutant to issue an order prohibiting the men from "selling United States stores that have been issued to them."

Meade made plans to have pontoon bridges span the Potomac River. He initially had three pontoon bridges with the army on the eve of the battle of Gettysburg, but had returned them to Washington. Now, he wanted them back. Four were soon on their way to Harpers Ferry.

By nightfall on July 6, Meade decided that Lee was heading for Hagerstown. He issued a circular laying out his army's routes to Middletown, on the edge of South Mountain. The army would begin heading toward its destination early on July 7. Meade considered merely following Lee's route, but worried that the Confederates could turn and attack. Additionally, the route strayed too far from his supply base. Meade's 30-hour delay gave Lee a head start—enough time to help ensure the Army of Northern Virginia made its way safely toward the Potomac River.

Not everyone was pleased with Meade's plans. Lincoln became Meade's most important critic. His discontent with Meade began days earlier when he read the army commander's July 4 congratulatory remarks to the troops. Lincoln told Halleck, "I did not like the phrase . . . 'Drive the invaders from our soil.'" Now he read that wounded Confederate soldiers were being ferried across the Potomac River and was dumbfounded that Meade seemed unwilling to stop it. He complained that the movements seemed "connected with a purpose to cover Baltimore and Washington and to get the enemy across the river again without a further collision, and they do not appear connected with a purpose to prevent his crossing and to destroy him."

Lincoln may have forgotten that the mantra for Meade and every other Army of the Potomac commander was to protect Washington and Baltimore at all costs. Lincoln's statement was the first time he advocated that the destruction of the Confederate army was paramount.

Cavalry Continue Clashing Over Wagons

Cavalry fights dominated July 6. Jeb Stuart chose not to follow Kilpatrick's Third Cavalry Division heading for Boonsboro. His orders were to screen Lee's retreating army, protect the precious wagon train, and not to battle the Union cavalry. Stuart now turned west to Leitersburg, Maryland, where he collected Jones's and Robertson's cavalry brigades, swelling his force to four brigades. Stuart's two other brigades, Hampton's (Baker's) and Fitz Lee's, were guarding Imboden's wagons rumbling toward Williamsport. General "Grumble" Jones, who was tangled up in fighting at Monterey Pass, rode to Williamsport to find his command, but learned it was at Leitersburg and galloped in its direction. When the men arrived, they observed the burned remains of scores of wagons—the result of the 1st Vermont Cavalry's attacks on Harman's train. Stuart's Confederate troopers were finally permitted a good night's rest, but this did not extend to their chief who, upon his arrival, waited all night for fresh orders from Lee. When they finally arrived at 6:00 a.m. on July 6, Stuart learned his men were to protect the wagons that had not yet reached Williamsport.

Stuart received reports of Kilpatrick and his men riding toward Boonsboro to reach the vulnerable wagons, rumbling through the streets of Hagerstown. The Confederate leader decided to split his command and take on Kilpatrick, who he knew to be too aggressive to allow the wagon train to continue its trek unscathed. Stuart sent Chambliss's and Robertson's troopers directly to Hagerstown to protect the train and designated his other two brigades as the force to contest Kilpatrick. Jenkins's brigade (now under Ferguson) was ordered to Chewsville, east of Hagerstown, and Grumble Jones's brigade headed south of the town to block the road from Funkstown. Stuart expected Jones to encounter Kilpatrick first, as Funkstown was on the direct route from Boonsboro.

Kilpatrick turned over hundreds of captured Confederates to Maj. Gen. William French on the evening of July 5, so he was now free of any impediments. French's scouts were also active, providing a stream of useful information to Meade and Washington. The most important observation may have been that the Confederates "could not cross the ford at Williamsport, the river being too high." French speculated an enemy move toward Falling Waters, about four miles downstream. According to historian Eric Wittenberg, "Whoever held Hagerstown, then, had the inside track to the critical fords that would carry Lee and his army to safety." Kilpatrick headed in that direction and a confrontation with Stuart before the end of the day. He later reported that upon "learning that Stuart was at Hagerstown, barricading the roads and entrenching his position to protect the large train near that place. . . . I marched early the following morning [July 6] to attack him." Kilpatrick remained interested in securing and destroying additional wagons.

As Kilpatrick led his division north on July 6, he learned Buford's First Division had crossed South Mountain at Turner's Gap and arrived in Boonsboro. William Gamble's and Thomas Devin's brigades, which saw hard fighting at Gettysburg, partially refitted at Westminster, and then headed to Frederick. Buford's third brigade, under Wesley Merritt, fought separately at Gettysburg on July 3, and was ordered to rejoin the division. Merritt's men had been in the saddle since 5:00 a.m. on July 4, heading west toward South Mountain. The horses were without fodder for almost five days, and hundreds broke down. They were left with their saddles on the side of the road. The now horseless troopers were forced to trudge along at the rear of Merritt's column. The division recombined on July 5, and Buford led the 3,500 men toward South Mountain the following morning to locate the Confederate wagons and determine how best to attack the train.

Kilpatrick decided to halt his division's movement toward Hagerstown and ride back to confer with Buford. They mutually agreed to work together: Kilpatrick to attack Stuart at Hagerstown; Buford to head to Williamsport to attack the thousands of

Colonel J. Lucius Davis commanded the 10th Virginia Cavalry during the fighting at Hagerstown where he was wounded and captured. Contemporaries called him "very sensitive and very courteous." (loc)

wagons hunkered down in the town. As Kilpatrick headed north, Buford put his division on the road to Williamsport at 4:00 a.m. These movements resulted in two distinct cavalry battles and two Union setbacks.

The Cavalry Fight at Hagerstown

As Colonel John Chambliss's brigade approached Hagerstown, he spun off the 9th Virginia Cavalry, sending it into town to determine if it was occupied by Union troopers. The Virginians did not initially see any enemy troops, but Kilpatrick's men soon began appearing west of town at about 1:30 p.m., after riding from Funkstown. Rain again pelted the area. Chambliss brought the rest of his brigade into town, halting at the town square. The 10th Virginia Cavalry, under Col. Lucius Davis, immediately began erecting a barricade across Potomac Street—one of the town's major thoroughfares. Colonel Nathaniel Richmond's Union brigade arrived first. Richmond spun off a handful of squadrons from the 18th Pennsylvania Cavalry and the 1st West Virginia Cavalry at 2:30 p.m. They quickly scattered the 9th Virginia Cavalry's picket line before crashing into the 10th Virginians' barricade. Although Confederate sharpshooters in church steeples picked off Richmond's men, they continued charging forward, driving the Virginians from their protective barrier.

Ulric Dahlgren, with about a hundred troopers from Gen. Wesley Merritt's cavalry brigade and a couple of companies of the 18th Pennsylvania Cavalry, battled the Confederates in the streets. He was grievously wounded in this vicinity. (lg)

General Beverly Robertson's brigade arrived next, but remained at a discrete distance from the fighting, as did the wagon train, which halted just north of town. Meanwhile, Richmond's victorious troopers continued riding deeper into Hagerstown, only to be hit by canister fire from three horse artillery batteries deployed near the town square. These cannon were supported by the remainder of Chambliss's brigade.

Kilpatrick brought up his artillery and shelled Chambliss's artillery. As the two sides banged away at each other, a 1st Maryland Cavalry (CSA) company counterattacked and drove Kilpatrick's troopers away from the Square. Chambliss sent a message to Stuart desperately requesting reinforcements. Stuart was already bringing up troops, as he may have seen an opportunity to destroy Richmond. While Chambliss's and Robertson's brigades directly faced the enemy, Stuart brought up Ferguson's brigade from the southeast and summoned Jones's brigade from the south. If coordinated, these movements could hit Richmond from three sides. However, Ferguson's threat was neutralized by elements of the 5th New York Cavalry and 1st Vermont Cavalry of Richmond's brigade, augmented by horse artillery.

Confederate cavalry hid behind fences and tombstones of the Zion Reformed Church during the battle of Hagerstown to fire on Union troops. Jonathan Hager, the founder of Hagerstown, also formed this church in 1770. (lg)

The afternoon saw a series of charges and countercharges as neither side could gain the upper hand. Daredevil Capt. Ulric Dahlgren, fresh from his attacks on Imboden's wagon train at Greencastle, decided to try another approach to drive the enemy from the town and capture the wagons. He dismounted a company of the 18th Pennsylvania Cavalry, placed men on either side of the street, and led them toward the town square to ambush the Confederates. They came under heavy fire, and Dahlgren received a severe leg wound necessitating amputation.

Chambliss pulled his men back from the square and formed another defensive line that repulsed additional Union attacks. Many of Chambliss's men used cemetery's headstones as cover as they banged away at enemy troopers. Elements of the 18th

Pennsylvania Cavalry and the 1st Vermont Cavalry made another attack, and the troopers of both sides hacked at each other in brutal hand-to-hand combat. The Union troopers were forced to withdraw when North Carolina infantrymen from Brig. Gen. Alfred Iverson's infantry brigade arrived and joined the cavalrymen in defense of Hagerstown.

This portion of Hagerstown was not developed when Union horse artillery was placed on this hill to pound the Confederates. (lg)

Custer's Michigan Wolverines arrived during the fighting and formed south of town, while Richmond skillfully shifted some of his troops to the southeast to face the threat from Ferguson's men. Iverson's infantry's arrival tipped the scales. Kilpatrick, who had fought unsuccessfully against Confederate infantry at Gettysburg on the afternoon of July 3, decided not to risk another encounter. He began withdrawing from Hagerstown by early evening, preventing Grumble Jones's men from attacking the Union rear. Kilpatrick blatantly misrepresented the fighting, writing in his report: "I moved on Hagerstown, and fell suddenly on Stuart, who, expecting me from the direction of Gettysburg, was surprised, routed, and driven toward Greencastle and Gettysburg." A *New York Times* reporter left a more accurate account of the battle, writing: "When the attack commenced, the fact was speedily discovered that there was a large force present, and it would be useless therefore to attempt to strike the train at this point, and General Kilpatrick decided to move rapidly to Williamsport." The fight in the Hagerstown

Brigadier General John Buford was a no-nonsense cavalry division commander whose reputation was cemented during the Gettysburg Campaign. He served with distinction until he died of typhoid fever in December 1863. (loc)

streets lasted about six hours and can be considered a Confederate victory, as Kilpatrick's men were denied the opportunity of destroying additional wagons.

Historian Eric Wittenberg and his colleagues argued that had "Kilpatrick held the place [Hagerstown] the previous day, this [Lee's] retreat route would have been blocked." It is hard to imagine how one Union cavalry division, numbering at most 3,000 men, could have blocked Lee's entire army.

The Cavalry Fight at Williamsport

General Imboden had carried out Lee's orders with a minimal loss of wagons. However, he had not bargained for heavy rains swelling the Potomac River, obliterating the fords in the area, nor the loss of the pontoon bridge. As a result, hundreds of Confederate wagons were sitting ducks with their backs against the river. Except for Imboden's cavalry brigade, the town was at the mercy of the Union troops descending on the area. Two other Confederate cavalry brigades remained with the wagon train, still rumbling toward Williamsport. Additional help was on the way. The 54th North Carolina, 58th Virginia, and a company from the 21st Virginia appeared on the Virginia side of the river and were ferried to Williamsport. These troops remained behind in Virginia to guard prisoners, collect stragglers, and later to guard ordnance trains. The men were tired from their 400-mile journey and their clothes and equipment were in poor condition. These troops were returning to Lee's army, but Imboden quickly pressed them into service.

Imboden received a report of a large body of Union cavalry—John Buford and his First Cavalry Division—heading in his direction. Reports of Kilpatrick's division at Hagerstown further darkened Imboden, who with fewer than 2,500 men now faced as many as 7,500 enemy troopers. He did have 26 cannon at his disposal, but most of their limber chests were almost empty. Imboden immediately began deploying his men in a semicircle around the town. By noon of July 6, he had augmented his defense by arming about 700 teamsters, and the wounded who could hold a rifle, into companies. He sent about 250 of these men to the right, a like number to the left, and retained the remainder in the center.

Buford's men appeared along three major roads leading to Williamsport (Williamsport-Hagerstown Pike, Williamsport-Boonsboro Pike, and Downsville Road) at about 1:30 p.m. The men had been in the saddle since 4:00 a.m. and were itching for a fight. Imboden later recalled, "[e]very man under my command understood that if we did not repulse the enemy we should all be captured and General Lee's army be ruined by the loss of its transportation, which at that period could not have been replaced in the Confederacy." While Buford knew of the massive array of wagons in Williamsport, he was not aware of the size of its defensive force.

Like George Custer, Brig. Gen. Wesley Merritt was a staff officer during the initial phases of the Civil War. Although only a captain, he jumped several grades to become a brigadier general in command of a cavalry brigade at Gettysburg. He grew into his role to become an effective cavalry leader. (loc)

Skirmishing first erupted near the College of St. James. The Confederates attacked first, when Capt. William Pegram launched his company of the 21st Virginia at Union cavalry along Downsville Road, south of Williamsport. The infantry drove Buford's troopers to the rear, but at the cost of Pegram's life. Imboden now ordered his artillery to open a rapid fire to confuse the enemy into thinking the town was well defended. It worked initially, but Imboden's cannon began running low on ammunition. Fortunately for Imboden, two wagons full of ammunition arrived from Winchester, which when ferried over the river allowed the artillery to spring back to life.

Buford deployed his troopers on either side of Williamsport-Boonsboro Pike: Wesley Merritt's brigade on the right of the road, William Gamble's on the left, and Tom Devin's brigade remained in reserve. Merritt pushed the 6th Pennsylvania Cavalry forward as a skirmish line, which forced Imboden back toward Williamsport. The Pennsylvanians' enthusiasm waned when the Confederate cannon in this sector redoubled their fire. The active Union artillery sent many shells falling among the wagons. The enslaved Black teamsters were nowhere to be found until someone gazed toward the river and saw "hundreds of black heads just showing above the water . . ." to escape the deadly fire.

Imboden now adopted a ploy to further confuse the enemy. Since only artillery was visible because of fire and smoke pouring out of their muzzles, he advanced his entire infantry, stretched in a single line, over a hundred yards in front of his artillery, in full view of Buford's cavalrymen. After waiting

awhile, Imboden pulled them back behind a hill. The charade worked, as Merritt thought he faced a strong enemy defense, which deterred him from attacking. To the south, Gamble's men pushed forward, capturing a couple dozen wagons that were collecting supplies. The Confederate artillery opened fire, pounding Gamble's men, and forcing them to break off the advance.

Gamble appeared more of a menace than Merritt, so Imboden transferred several units from his left to the right, advancing them toward the dismounted Union troopers. Eight of Imboden's Napoleon cannons, under the command of Maj. Benjamin Eshleman, galloped forward 400 yards, dropped trail, and fired into Gamble's vulnerable left flank, throwing it in disarray, and forcing the cavalrymen to pull back. Merritt also began his advance, so Imboden moved six cannon forward several hundred yards to fire into the enemy's right flank. At the same time, Imboden launched his remaining defensive line on the left, the 58th Virginia and a handful of companies of the 54th North Carolina, against Merritt.

About this time, Imboden received a message from Fitz Lee, "telling me to 'hold my own' as he would be up in half hour with three thousand fresh men. The news was sent along our whole line, and was received with a wild and exultant yell. We knew then that the field was won, and [we] slowly pressed forward." Buford's men could hear Fitz Lee's cannon firing in the distance, which dulled their enthusiasm.

Fitz Lee's men galloped along Greencastle Road as night fell, finally lifting the siege. As Lee's men prepared to launch into Merritt's exposed right flank, Buford ordered his buglers to sound the withdrawal. Devin's men, who had been held in reserve, formed the rearguard.

The July 6 setbacks of Buford and Kilpatrick were not yet over. While Kilpatrick claimed he immediately set off for Williamsport to assist Buford, the latter told a different, and probably more accurate, story. Buford claimed he put his men back on the road to Boonsboro, reaching it at about midnight, but was delayed by "Kilpatrick's division having been driven back in confusion from the direction of Hagerstown, completely blockading the road in our rear, making it impassable for several hours."

During the early part of his division's retreat, Kilpatrick heard gunfire between Merritt's and Imboden's troops at Williamsport and worried about the safety of his division making its way south. He spun off Custer's brigade, sending it down the Williamsport-Hagerstown Pike toward the sound of battle. Custer deployed his regiments on either side of the pike about halfway to Williamsport but did not remain there long. Confederate artillery opened fire on the exposed troops, causing considerable confusion. Custer retraced his steps and joined Kilpatrick's column moving south. The Confederate troopers that had faced Kilpatrick at Hagerstown were unwilling to allow him to get away unscathed, so they closely followed. Colonel Richmond's 1st West Virginia, supported by Elder's battery, formed the rearguard. It was forced to halt several times to engage the enemy. This series of encounters continued into the night.

The fight for the wagons had now ended. July 6 proved to be a bloody day for both sides. Kent Masterson Brown called it a "fiasco" for the Union cavalry. The fighting in front of Williamsport removed almost a hundred men from Buford's ranks and 125 from Imboden's. Kilpatrick lost 175 men at Hagerstown, and Stuart lost more than 200. Although Lee's wagons were now safe, his army was still vulnerable, stretching about 18 miles from Fairfield, Pennsylvania, to near Hagerstown, Maryland.

The Armies in Motion

CHAPTER FIVE

JULY 7, 1863

Washingtonians broke out in wild celebration when they learned on July 7 of Vicksburg's capture. After years of frustration, the twin victories at Vicksburg and Gettysburg lifted the malaise. Upon hearing the news, Secretary of the Navy Gideon Welles headed to the Executive Mansion to inform Lincoln. A *Sacramento Union* correspondent noted Lincoln "never before or afterward saw Mr. Welles so thoroughly excited as he was then." Lincoln and others now turned their attention north to Maryland, where Lee's beaten army appeared trapped against the river and ripe for destruction. The correspondent wrote, "We are in almost hourly expectation of a great battle which should be fought on Maryland soil and result in the annihilation of the army of Virginia [sic] and the hastening of the collapse of the rebellion."

In western Maryland, torrential rains continued soaking men and beasts on July 7. Buford's and Kilpatrick's divisions arrived at Boonsboro after midnight, and the men were overjoyed to be given a day's rest. The same was not true of Tom Devin's

Built in 1732, the Old South Mountain Inn sits atop Turner's Gap through South Mountain. General Edward Braddock's command probably marched past the inn on its way to western Pennsylvania. Confederate Maj. Gen. Daniel Harvey Hill made it his headquarters during the fighting on September 14, 1862, during the Maryland Campaign. The property became the summer home of Madeleine Dahlgren, wife of Adm. John Dahlgren, in the late 1800s. (lg)

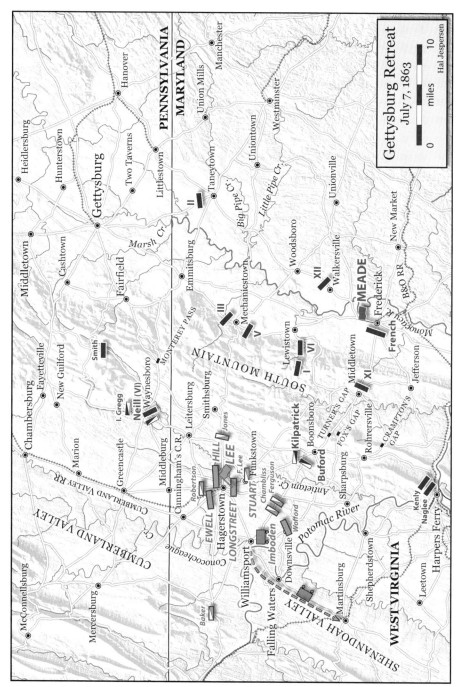

JULY 7—Lee reached Hagerstown as Meade's men pursued from three directions. Union troops from other commands also converged on Hagerstown, making Lee's position most vulnerable.

brigade, which remained near Williamsport to cover the retreat. When Stuart learned of this tantalizing opportunity to pounce on an isolated brigade, he marshaled his men and marched east. Devin skirmished with Stuart's men until receiving orders to pull back. Stuart's troopers closely followed, forcing Devin into a fighting retreat.

The Last of Lee's Army Reaches Hagerstown

Lee and his battered army continued their miserable march early on the morning of July 7. By the end of the day, the entire Confederate infantry were in and around Hagerstown, less than seven miles from the Potomac River. Because of Meade's reluctance to actively pursue until he was sure of his adversary's intentions, Lee was able to get a head start, reaching his destination almost unscathed. Lee lost hundreds of wagons, thousands of men, and needed supplies, but got his army and the lion's share of wagons safely to their destination. A quandary now faced him as the river rose to about 13 feet and no bridges spanned the Potomac River. Imboden supervised the placement of a second ferry boat to move wounded men across the river. The new additional boat was hardly enough to transport thousands of men and wagons. Those that remained in Williamsport were sickened by the stench from thousands of horses and unwashed men.

The men of Ewell's corps were the last of Lee's troops to reach Hagerstown. They left Waynesboro at daylight and set a fast pace, reaching Leitersburg by noon, and continuing to their destination. They encountered thousands of captured Union troops guarded by Pickett's division about two miles out of Hagerstown. A brass band struck up "Dixie" and "Yankee Doodle" to entertain the captives. A New York officer spied Lee sitting quietly nearby and recalled he exuded a "quiet dignity, strongly at variance with the boisterous mirth of the young men around him . . . he looked as he might on the gambles of so many kittens." Ewell's men camped just north of Hagerstown on the Hagerstown-Waynesboro Pike, where they could protect Lee's left flank and rear.

Men could rest while Lee established his headquarters outside Hagerstown on Antietam

Nicknamed "Father Neptune," Gideon Welles served as secretary of the Navy through the Civil War and into 1869. His diary is a gold mine of information on the war and life in Lincoln's Cabinet. (loc)

Colonel Tom Devin entered the war as a house painter, but he quickly rose through the cavalry ranks to command a brigade at Gettysburg. He was a favorite of John Buford and earned the nickname "Buford's hard hitter." He later assumed command of a cavalry division. (loc)

Many Northern publications dramatized Lee's retreat across the Potomac River. This drawing shows some of Lee's men reaching the Virginia shore. (bjl)

Creek. There he considered how to get his army across the swollen Potomac River. He worried about several other issues while here. Would Meade attack? In anticipation, Lee told his men to prepare "for an engagement which may be expected at any time." Men were also told to get ready for an influx of ammunition as ordnance wagons arrived on the Virginia side of the river about 2:00 p.m. on July 5. The precious commodity was ferried across the Potomac River. The army also direly needed horses to replace those lost during the battle and the retreat, so Lee sent details out to collect them from nearby farms with payment in Confederate currency. Those officers and men unauthorized to hold horses would be required to relinquish them to the artillery.

Confederate quartermasters continued plying their trade by scouring the countryside for supplies. Longstreet's corps alone on July 7 collected 18,400 pounded of hay, over 525 bushels of corn, 460 pounds of coal, 23 bushels of oats, and 16 horses. The take was probably even higher as it only tallied Hood's and part of McLaws's divisions. The hungry men also roamed around Hagerstown and the surrounding countryside looking for food. Lee was forced to deploy his provost guards to prevent looting. A chaplain in the 28th North Carolina noted that "Gen'l Lee is trying hard to prevent incidents of that sort [looting] but I am sorry to say he has not been successful." Even the provost guard participated in the looting, and an officer in the 47th Virginia became intoxicated on stolen whisky and arrested.

Union Troops Converge on Lee's Army

Lee learned he was up against more than the Army of the Potomac. Troops from the Departments of West Virginia and Susquehanna were converging on Hagerstown, as was a large contingent from Maj. Gen. Samuel Heintzelman's Washington garrison. The army could soon be boxed in on three sides, and if not vigilant, surrounded. Lee suspected Washington was pressuring the various commands to pursue and destroy him and his army. For example, when Brig. Gen. Benjamin Kelley reported on July 5th it would take several days for him to concentrate his men and begin their move into Maryland, Secretary of War Edwin Stanton lambasted him, writing, "It will be a matter of deep regret if, by tardy movement, you let the chance escape. There should be no rest, night or day. Why are you still in Clarksburg [West Virginia]? This communication was followed by several others by Gen. Halleck, attempting to hasten Kelley along. These communications had the desired impact on Kelley as he immediately pushed toward Maryland.

Major General Samuel Heintzelman commanded one of the Union army corps during the early part of the Civil War, but was eclipsed by many of his subordinates, such as Philip Kearny and Joseph Hooker. Not a particularly aggressive fighter, he was removed from field command after the Second Bull Run Campaign and was assigned command of the Washington defenses. (loc)

Back at Frederick, George Meade and his staff established new headquarters at the United States Hotel during the afternoon of July 7. He "was received with much enthusiasm by the people of Frederick and the soldiers," noted a newspaper correspondent. Meade did not like this adoration, but gritted his teeth and gracefully tried to accept the proffered plaudits. He wrote to his wife on July 8 about how the "people in this place have made a great fuss with me. . . . The street has been crowded with people, staring at me, and, much to my astonishment, I find myself a lion." He continued, "I cannot say I appreciate all this honor . . . because I feel certain it is undeserved, and would like people to wait a little while."

Edwin Stanton played a hands-on role as secretary of war in Lincoln's cabinet. A favorite of the Radical Republicans, Stanton was a superb organizer, but many thought he was a micromanager. (loc)

Soon after his arrival, Meade received a telegram from Halleck, informing him he had been "appointed a brigadier-general in the Regular Army, to rank from July 3, the date of your brilliant victory at Gettysburg." Halleck's actions may have had merit, but some have speculated it may have been the "carrot" to get Meade moving toward Lee's destruction. Perhaps to emphasize his oft-stated position, Halleck wrote to Meade later that evening: "You have given the enemy a stunning blow at Gettysburg. Follow it up, and give him another before he can reach the Potomac."

July 7 found Meade's units making exhausting marches, usually beginning a few hours after midnight. The army split into pieces, each taking a different route to Middletown, between Catoctin Mountain to the east and South Mountain to the west. The army marched from two major points.

Marching Through Emmitsburg

The I Corps marched 15 miles that day, beginning the day at Emmitsburg and ending at Hamburg atop Catoctin Mountain.

The III Corps began its march at Gettysburg, and its 21-mile march brought it to Mechanicstown (Thurmont).

The V Corps also began the day at Emmitsburg, and beginning at 6:00 a.m., marched 17 miles to bivouac at Utica, about five miles from Frederick.

Sedgwick's VI Corps did not leave Emmitsburg until 11:00 a.m. and marched about 11 hours toward Hamburg.

Howard's XI Corps had the longest march, beginning at Emmitsburg and ending about 30 miles after reaching Middletown.

From the South/Littlestown

The II Corps began southeast of Gettysburg, marching 11 miles through Littlestown to Taneytown.

The XII Corps, already at Littlestown, marched to Walkersville, about seven miles northeast of Frederick.

Major General Carl Schurz's division (XI Corps) reached Middletown first, at 11:00 p.m. on July 7. The army's other units were not far behind on the east side of Catoctin Mountain.

When the troops reached Middletown, they were joined by their quartermaster and subsistence trains, parked near Westminster, Maryland, during the battle. The trains were now making their way to Frederick and then on to rendezvous with their respective corps. In the meantime, the men had to fend for themselves, so they stripped the countryside bare of food, forage, and any other supplies needed. A reporter noted how every establishment and house in Frederick "and all

Major General Carl Schurz had a distinguished career prior to the Civil War. A German revolutionary, he emigrated to the United States and became a statesman, journalist, and reformer. Lincoln needed to cultivate the German vote, so he elevated Schurz to the rank of general. (loc)

Another one of Edwin Forbes's illustrations showing the Union pursuit in the driving rain. (loc)

the surrounding towns through which the army passed, have been completely eaten out, stripped of everything edible and biblible. . . . The crops are abundant, but the men can't eat hay, straw and raw corn."

A soldier noted, "It has been raining all day and bids fair to rain all night . . . the men's rations are exhausted and [if] this is the rate at which we are going to cross the mountains, we are going to have a starving time." The men were miserable; however, cheering civilians along their route boosted their morale. A member of the 13th Massachusetts never forgot a group of "pretty bright-eyed girls, all dressed in 'Stars and Stripes' . . . forming themselves into a group ... waving a flag, they sung the 'Battle-Cry of Freedom.'" He recalled hardened veterans' "eyes moistened as they listened in silence to the words of that noble hymn. It was a graceful thing, which the lapse of time cannot efface from our memory." The historian of the 37th Massachusetts recalled how many "had been the demonstrations of delight along the route by the loyal people, some of whom came from miles away to look upon the valiant veterans who had freed them from the presence of the hated foe."

Meade solved a nettlesome issue on July 7 when he incorporated Maj. Gen. French's novice division from Harpers Ferry into the army's III Corps. The corps was leaderless because of the wounding of Maj. Gen. Dan Sickles at Gettysburg on July 2, and French assumed command. The III Corps veterans were not welcoming of the new arrivals. Brigade commander Col. Philippe de Trobriand noted that what "the Third Corps gained in numbers it lost in homogeneity . . . the new-comers were never fully naturalized in the corps."

Meade Makes Progress

CHAPTER SIX
JULY 8, 1863

Lee pondered his next steps, as the entire Confederate army rested in and around Hagerstown. Lee decided to protect his troops by creating a stout defensive line, should Meade attack while they were pinned against the Potomac River. Lee spent most of the day in the saddle, reconnoitering the area to determine where best to lay out his line.

General John Imboden continued caring for men and wagons around Williamsport. Two ferries persisted, moving wounded across the river to ambulances on the opposite side. Prisoners were also a priority. Officers and enlisted men were separated; the former were sent across first. One of the ferry wires broke, considerably reducing flow across the river until repaired. Imboden had already solved the issue of food for the men as he "required every family in the town to cook provisions for the wounded, under pain of having its kitchen occupied," according to an artillery officer. During return trips, the ferry carried food, supplies, and ordnance to Lee's army. The supply

Wagons, axle to axle, filled this space between the C&O Canal and the Potomac River. You can see the canal in the foreground of the photo. (lg)

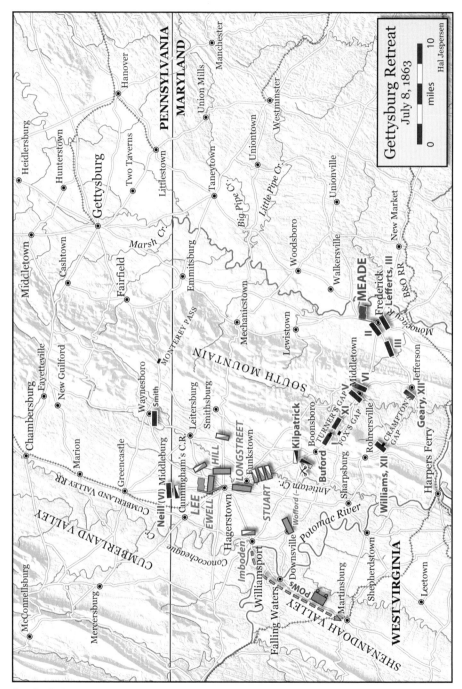

JULY 8—As Lee pondered how best to lay out his defensive works near Hagerstown, the Union army converged on Middletown, Maryland. Stuart's attacks on the Union cavalry near Boonsboro attempted to keep them away from Lee's right flank, as the Federal infantry began crossing South Mountain and inched closer to the Confederate army.

of ammunition was so dire that ammunition wagons continued galloping to the river from Winchester without a guard.

A Frustrated Meade Deals with Washington

The telegraph wires between Meade's headquarters and Washington heated up on July 8 as Lincoln became increasingly frustrated by the Army of the Potomac's slow progress. Meade updated Halleck on his situation during the early afternoon. The candid message informed, provided rationales, and attempted to tamp down unrealistic expectations.

He began this communication with an update on the condition of the army:

After a moderately successful military career during the early stages of the Civil War, Maj. Gen. Henry Halleck became the general-in-chief of all U.S. armies in the field. His non-confrontational style and reluctance to provide decisive orders to army commanders frustrated Lincoln, who referred to him as a glorified secretary. He was replaced by U. S. Grant in 1864. (loc)

The rains of yesterday and last night have made all roads but- [turn]pikes almost impassable. Artillery and wagons are stalled; it will take time to collect them together. . . . A large portion of the men are barefooted. Shoes will arrive at Frederick to-day, and will be issued as soon as possible. . . . The spirit of the army is high; the men are ready and willing to make every exertion to push forward.

Next, he tried to reassure Halleck that he had every intention of following and perhaps engaging Lee:

The very first moment I can get the different commands, the artillery and cavalry, properly supplied and in hand, I will move forward. . . . Be assured I most earnestly desire to try the fortunes of war with the enemy on this side of the river. . . .

However, he sought to temper Halleck's (and Lincoln's) expectations:

I expect to find the enemy in a strong position, well covered with artillery, and I do not desire to imitate his example at Gettysburg, and assault a position where the chances were so greatly against success. . . . I wish in advance to moderate the expectations of those who, in ignorance of the difficulties to be encountered, may expect too much. All that I can do under the circumstances I pledge this army to do.

Rain was pervasive during the early stages of the march, soaking the men to the skin and making many roads almost impassible. (loc)

All of Meade's comments were accurate. General Howard informed Meade of the dire shoe and sock situation—about "one-half of my command are now destitute, or have shoes too poor to march." Howard held them back, explaining the "remainder of the corps will march as soon as provisions arrive," which he expected very soon. A VI Corps aide wrote how the roads "are frightful . . . [the batteries] have been trying all day to get over [the mountain gaps]. It will take until tomorrow noon before [they] are entirely across, and then the horses will be unfit for use."

The infantry was miserable marching through the muck. Most had not eaten all day because the provision wagons had not yet arrived. At least the rain ended in the afternoon. The historian of the 124th New York recounted how the III Corps marched through Frederick on July 8, the "most unsoldierly, sorry looking victorious veteran army. . . . For two days we had been spattering each other with mud and slush, and soaked with rain which was falling in torrents. Our guns and swords were covered with rust; our pockets were filled with dirt. . . ."

Meade was not in much better shape. He wrote to his wife, "from the time I took command till to-day, now over ten days, I have not changed my clothes, have not had a regular night's rest, and many nights not a wink of sleep, and for several days did not even wash my face and hands, no regular food, and all the time in a great state of mental anxiety. Indeed, I think I have not lived as much in this time as in the last thirty years."

As Meade was preparing his message to Halleck, the Union general-in-chief, apparently under pressure from Lincoln, wrote to the general. He told Meade he had received "reliable information that the enemy is crossing at Williamsport. The opportunity to attack his divided forces should not be lost. The President is urgent and anxious that your army should move against him by forced marches."

Meade knew better and replied, "My information as to the crossing of the enemy does not agree with that just received in your dispatch." He correctly told Halleck, "His whole force [Lee's] is between Funkstown and Williamsport," and added, "[m]y army is and has been making forced marches, short of rations, and barefooted. One corps marched yesterday and last night over 30 miles. I take occasion to repeat that I will use my utmost efforts to push forward this army."

Realizing he was dealing with a sensitive army commander, Halleck quickly penned a response:

> *Do not understand me as expressing any dissatisfaction; on the contrary, your army has done most nobly. I only wish to give you opinions formed from information received here. It is telegraphed from near Harper's Ferry that the enemy have been crossing for the last two days. It is also reported that they have a bridge across. If Lee's army is so divided by the river, the importance of attacking the part on this side is incalculable. Such an opportunity may never occur again. If, on the contrary, he has massed his whole force on the Antietam, time must be taken to also concentrate your forces. Your opportunities for information are better than mine. . . . You will have forces sufficient to render your victory certain. My only fear now is that the enemy may escape by crossing the river.*

The Cavalry Fight Near Boonsboro

Jeb Stuart worried that Alfred Pleasonton planned to send his cavalry to harass the Confederate Army around Hagerstown, so he concentrated his force at Funkstown, between Hagerstown and Boonsboro. Stuart noted in his campaign report how he advanced from Funkstown toward Boonsboro, "on the different roads, in order, by a bold demonstration, to threaten an advance upon the enemy, and thus cover the retrograde of the main [army] body." He did not know Pleasonton's orders were merely to protect the South Mountain gaps for use by the Union infantry. Boonsboro was important as it was strategically placed at the base of the mountain.

Grumble Jones's Confederate cavalry brigade led the advance along the National Road toward Boonsboro, with Stuart's other brigades riding behind it. A Union signal station atop South Mountain observed these movements, so Buford and Kilpatrick, who were screening the infantry's movement toward Lee's army, could prepare for an attack. Buford's men were camped west of Boonsboro along Beaver Creek, on the National Road—directly in the path of Stuart's advance. Kilpatrick's men rested on the east side of the town.

Buford deployed Gamble's and Merritt's brigades on the right of the National Road with Devin's brigade in reserve. After surveying the strong Union position, Stuart decided on a flanking movement, bringing up Ferguson's brigade along the Williamsport-Boonsboro Road to the right. Buford needed assistance, so Kilpatrick mounted his men and rode to his aid. He also sent Devin's brigade to counter the Confederate advance.

Grumble Jones organized the Confederate counter by dismounting his men, sending them toward the Union line, followed by three other brigades. Ferguson also dismounted his brigade, and it began pushing back Devin's troopers. Stuart unleashed several mounted attacks, which initially caused the Union line to fall back as Kilpatrick arrived to attempt to stem the Confederate advance.

Meade became aware of the deteriorating situation and sent infantry from the VI and XI Corps pouring over South Mountain to bolster Pleasonton's line. A Confederate artilleryman explained, "[l]ate this evening the Yankee cavalry was reinforced by infantry, and then they in turn drove us back about a mile, and to the same position we had when the fight commenced." Stuart wisely pulled back to Funkstown, but not before Gamble's brigade launched an attack, which hastened the retreat. Stuart had succeeded in his mission of tying up the enemy's cavalry, thus protecting Lee's right flank as the men continued

developing their defensive line. Each side lost about 80 men during the fight.

Getting from Middletown, across South Mountain, and into Boonsboro took its toll on the XI Corps. One of its soldiers explained how he thought it was "the longest day I ever saw. We had to cross a range of mountains. It commenced raining about six o'clock and was so dark we could hardly see anything. Some of the boys would fall down in the mud but get up again laughing and trudge along."

This woodcut dramatizes the cavalry action at Boonsboro, where most of Jeb Stuart's Confederate troopers attacked John Buford's and Judson Kilpatrick's cavalry divisions. The timely appearance of Union infantry helped convince Stuart to break off the fight and head toward Hagerstown. (loc)

Meade's Men Continue
Their Trek Toward Lee's Army

Dawn on July 8 saw Meade's entire infantry on the road, making their way toward a rendezvous with Lee's army.

The I Corps left the small village of Hamburg (which some soldiers renamed "Humbug") and marched to Middletown, where it rested for a few hours, and then continued to Turner's Gap in South Mountain—a march of about 18 miles. The fighting at Boonsboro rattled new corps commander John Newton, so he ordered his men to build crude entrenchments on the south side of the gap to protect against "a threatened attack by the enemy."

The II Corps, bivouacked at Taneytown, Maryland, marched 20 miles and stopped for the night within about six miles of Frederick.

Civilization has impinged on much of the Boonsboro battlefield, but some areas remain undeveloped. Several charges occurred across this field. (lg)

The III Corps at Mechanicstown (Thurmont), Maryland, marched 18 to 23 miles to the outskirts of Frederick.

The V Corps marched from Utica and crossed over Catoctin Mountain to Middletown, arriving about 4 p.m. Some units marched close to 20 miles.

Sedgwick's VI Corps reached Middletown between 9 a.m. and noon.

Howard's XI Corps began the day in Middletown, and climbed South Mountain. Some units continued toward Boonsboro to support the Union cavalry.

The XII Corps began its march at 4:30 a.m. from Walkersville and scaled South Mountain at Crampton's Gap after the 13-hour march that covered 17 miles.

By the end of July 8, two of Meade's corps (the V and XI) were a mere 12 miles from Lee's army, and the rest were not far behind. Historian Kent Masterson Brown called Meade's journey "incredibly fast." As many as half of Meade's men were shoeless by this time, and all were muddy, exhausted, and soaked to the skin.

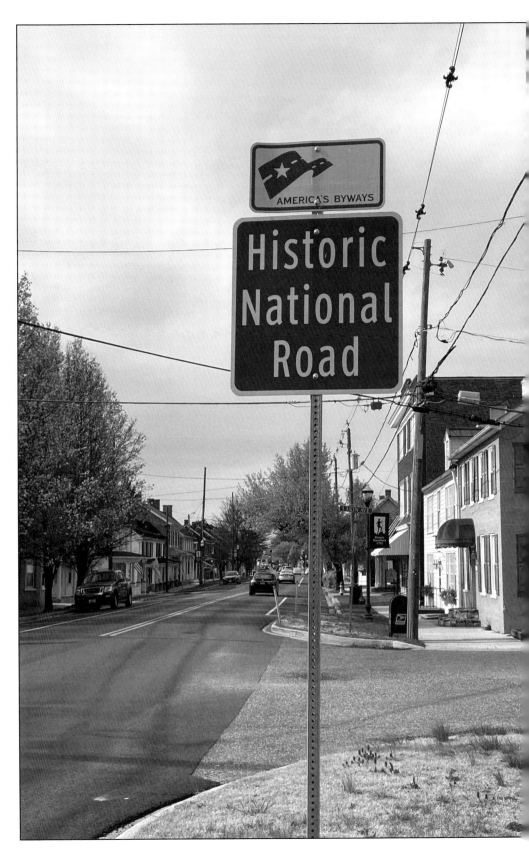

Lee's Defensive Line

CHAPTER SEVEN

JULY 9, 1863

July 9 dawned cloudy, but no rains soaked the men and animals for the first time in days. Soon, the day became hot and humid. With the Potomac River unwilling to recede, Lee focused on creating a sound defensive position.

Lee left his headquarters, about two miles below Hagerstown, and rode north until noon with his three corps commanders, engineers, chief mapmaker, and a trusted artillery chief. He finally settled on Salisbury Ridge as his defensive position. The ridge rose almost 150 feet above Marsh Run, and ran in a north-south direction through Hagerstown. Unfortunately, the ridge was not uniform and was broken up in several areas. "There was no very well defined & naturally strong line," noted artilleryman Col. Edward Porter Alexander, "& we had to pick & choose, & string together in some places by make-shifts & some little work." The right flank of the 15-mile line was anchored near the Potomac River at Downsville. The line then snaked north, passing by St. James College, and its left flank rested on Conochocheague Creek. Any attack

The National Road, shown here in Boonsboro, Maryland, was the first major road designed, funded, and built by the Federal government. Constructed between 1811 and 1837, the 620-mile road was a major thoroughfare for settlers traveling west. (lg)

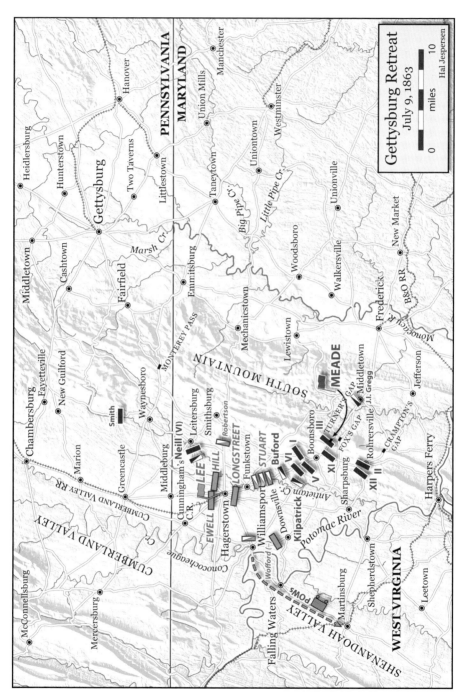

Gettysburg Retreat
July 9, 1863

0   miles   10

Hal Jespersen

July 9—As Lee's men busied themselves creating their strong defensive positions near Hagerstown, the Union army approached. It was an uncharacteristically quiet day for the Union cavalry.

against Lee's defensive line required the enemy to cross several small ridges, traverse muddy bottomlands, and wade Marsh Run before getting to Salisbury Ridge. The position was so important that Lee, an engineer by training, oversaw the layout and construction of the line. Hospitals were created behind the front line in anticipation of the coming fight.

The task of ferrying the Confederate wounded and Union prisoners across the Potomac continued on July 9. The second ferry boat was put back into action, and engineers collected four canal boats and began ferrying men across the river in the small craft. Williamsport became an unhealthy cesspool. The streets flooded, and thousands of men and as many as 30,000 horses and mules soiled the area. Fortunately, most of the captured herds of cattle, sheep, and pigs had already been transported across the river, but hundreds had perished during the journey.

Union signal stations were well-used by the Union army during the war. This illustration shows a soldier watching Lee's army, and the legs above him are probably a soldier's who is communicating this information to the army via signal flags. (loc)

The Union Army Begins Assembling in Front of Lee

The Union Army again took up the march on July 9, although it traveled shorter distances than the day before. Meade sent a long message to Halleck about his situation at 11:00 a.m.:

> *The army is moving in three columns, the right column having in it three corps. The line occupied to-day with the advance will be on the other side of the mountains, from Boonsborough to Rohrersville. . . . The enemy's infantry were driven back yesterday evening from Boonsborough, or, rather, they retired on being pressed toward Hagerstown.*

The missive continued:

> *[The] state of the river and the difficulty of crossing has rendered it imperative on him [Lee] to have his army, artillery, and trains ready to receive my attack. I propose to move on a line from Boonsborough toward*

Both armies foraged extensively after the battle of Gettysburg. This sketch shows Union soldiers collecting hay. (loc)

the center of the [Lee's] line from Hagerstown to Williamsport, my left flank looking to the river and my right toward the mountains, keeping the road to Frederick in my rear and center. I shall try to keep as concentrated as the roads by which I can move will admit, so that, should the enemy attack, I can move to meet him, and, if he assumes the defensive, I can deploy as I think proper.

Halleck agreed about Lee's position and told Meade not to be "influenced by any dispatch from here against your judgment." With this message, Meade could put his full attention toward maneuvering against Lee.

By the end of the day, Meade's army had crept closer to Lee. Meade moved his headquarters to Turner's Gap from Middletown, where he joined the I and XI Corps, already in front of Lee's army. A mile

Because the Union VI Corps was the last of Meade's army to arrive at Gettysburg, it was tasked with leading the pursuit. This Edwin Forbes illustration shows it crossing Antietam Creek at Funkstown. (loc)

south, the III Corps reached Fox's Gap and prepared to bivouac. Four of Meade's corps passed over South Mountain and spent the night on its west side: The V and VI Corps were at Boonsboro; the II and XII Corps were about six miles south at Rohrersville, Maryland. Buford's cavalry division drew rations and then skirmished with Confederate cavalry near Funkstown. Kilpatrick's troopers remained near Boonsboro until the afternoon, when they rode north to support Buford's men.

Meade Prepares to Attack

CHAPTER EIGHT
JULY 10, 1863

Few soldiers probably realized they had crossed the Mason-Dixon line during their march from Gettysburg. Survey work for the line determining the boundary between Maryland and Pennsylvania began in 1765, but problems plagued the project, and the line of markers was not completed until 1784. (lg)

Lee concentrated on finishing his defensive line and laying a pontoon bridge over the Potomac on July 10. By late afternoon, he began maneuvering his men into position. The army did not complete this movement until July 11. Not only was Lee confronting Meade's approaching army, but he also received reports of Smith's division at Waynesboro and Neill's brigade at Leitersburg. They were heading toward his left flank at Hagerstown. Benjamin Kelley's 6,000-man Army of West Virginia approached his rear. Time was growing short, as Lee directed all the corps' pioneers to head over to Falling Waters to assist in building the bridge.

Although in dire straits as the Union Army maneuvered into position for the showdown, Lee continued ordering foraging parties to comb the area. Early on July 10, he sent a company from each brigade to collect livestock, wagons, and supplies.

After sustaining such a devastating defeat at Gettysburg, Southerners were concerned about the

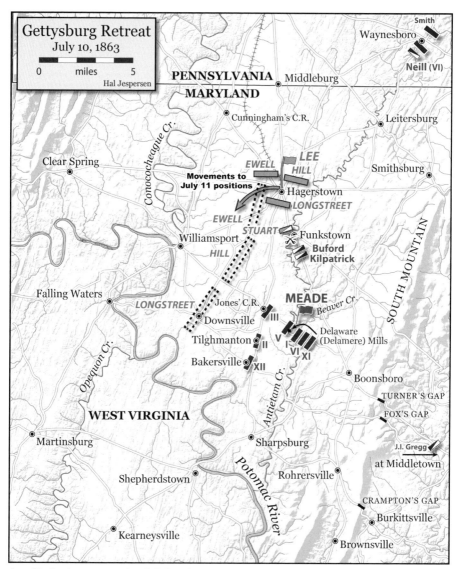

JULY 10—Lee's men completed their defensive works as Meade continued moving into position. The Union cavalry probed the Confederate line toward Funkstown and battled Stuart's horsemen. Infantry from both armies entered the fighting here.

condition of Lee's army. Lee assured Pres. Jefferson Davis that the "army is in good condition, and we have a good supply of ammunition." Others were not so sure. Capt. Fitzgerald Ross, a foreign national traveling with Lee's army, called the men a "demoralized horde of fugitives." He believed Meade would lose all credibility if he did not "capture the whole crowd."

The Union Army Continues
Moving into Position to Confront Lee

Lee was running out of time as the Union Army pushed through South Mountain and poured into the valley beyond. The march of various infantry corps differed in duration and intensity on July 10. Most were short, averaging only eight miles. By the end of the day, Meade had three of his corps facing Lee's right flank: The III Corps formed on the army's right, bisecting the Boonsboro-Williamsport Pike at Jones' Crossroads after a series of marches from just west of Turner's Gap. Its troops experienced a most difficult July 10. After traveling about five miles during the day, the men bivouacked about a mile from Little Antietam Creek at 7:15 p.m. They broke camp at 10:50 p.m., and after recrossing Antietam Creek, again bivouacked, this time at 3:00 a.m. near the Boonsborough-Williamsport Turnpike. The men did not remain here long, as they were ordered back into line and marched another five miles, where they finally camped in a large wheat field.

The president of the Confederacy, Jefferson Davis, should have been the ideal commander-in-chief. A West Point graduate, he served as secretary of war in the Franklin Pierce administration. However, he proved to be less effective than Abraham Lincoln in this role. (loc)

The II Corps remained at Tilghmanton. It had the longest march—12 miles—beginning near Crampton's Gap. The men observed decaying graves from the battle of Antietam, remarking on the sight of bones protruding from shallow graves. The XII Corps formed the left at Bakersville. Like the II Corps, it began its march at Crampton's Gap and marched 12 miles to its destination. Cpl. E. R. Brown of the 27th Indiana was struck by the similarity of the route from a year earlier, during the Maryland Campaign. He noted that it was another "object lesson to us that, 'It is the unexpected that happens in war.'"

The four remaining corps were stacked along the Boonsboro-Williamsport Pike behind the III Corps. The V Corps began its march near Boonsboro, crossed Antietam Creek, and bivouacked near Beaver Creek. The I Corps marched through Boonsboro, heading northwest toward Beaver Creek, where it threw up earthworks. Most of the VI Corps came next, only marching three miles from Boonsboro and then crossing Antietam Creek. Some units were thrown north to support Buford's cavalry at Funkstown. Howard's XI Corps occupied the rear, near the VI

Several Confederate units crossed this bridge over Antietam Creek during the battle of Funkstown, which featured considerable fighting by both the infantry and cavalry. (lg)

Corps, about two and a half miles from Funkstown, near the Hagerstown-Smoketown Road. Buford's First Cavalry Division roamed around Lee's right flank and reported Lee's position stretching between Hagerstown and Jones' Crossroads. Kilpatrick's Third Division, which had been riding and fighting almost nonstop since before the battle of Gettysburg, rested near Lee's left flank. Because Lee was massing in the front of his army, Meade urged caution, telling his corps commanders to "keep themselves in communication with the columns on the right and left, and be prepared to move forward if the developments of the day should require." Meade made his headquarters at the Mountain House atop Turner's Gap.

Meade's intelligence arm provided an accurate stream of information. Thomas Ryan and Richard Schaus criticized Meade for inactivity because of an "obvious misreading of, or lack of reaction to, intelligence indicating Lee's army had not yet taken up its new position." Meade wrote Halleck on the afternoon of July 10, "I shall advance cautiously on the same line tomorrow until I can develop more fully the enemy's force and position, upon which my future operations will depend."

Halleck made a 180-degree turn that evening, writing, "I think it will be best for you to postpone a general battle till you can concentrate all your forces and get up your reserves and reinforcements. I will push on the troops as fast as they arrive. . . . They should join you by forced marches. Beware of partial combats. Bring up and hurl upon the enemy all your forces, good and bad." After days of pushing Meade, this message must have surprised and somewhat baffled him.

Reinforcements were beginning to arrive. Smith's division was an important addition, but was in rough shape after its march from Carlisle. The men were soaked to the skin, many were shoeless, and all were covered with mud and famished as the supply trains were miles in the rear. When they finally united with the Army of the Potomac, they were attached to the VI Corps.

Battle of Funkstown

Stuart pulled back toward Funkstown after battling Buford and Kilpatrick at Boonsboro on July 8. Only four miles south of Hagerstown, and east of the growing Confederate defensive line, Funkstown held strategic value to both armies. Buford received orders to saddle up his division and capture the town on July 10. He approached from the southeast with his three brigades as Stuart deployed his five brigades in a wide semicircle encompassing the southern and eastern portions of the town. The troopers did not have long to wait as Buford's men approached at a

Several homes that stood during the battle of Funkstown remain intact. This includes the Hudson house. (lg)

Robert E. Lee's nephew, Brig. Gen. Fitzhugh Lee, served in the cavalry through the war. Although he commanded a brigade during the Gettysburg Campaign, he later commanded a cavalry division and was considered for command of the cavalry after J. E. B. Stuart's death. The position ultimately went to Wade Hampton. (loc)

"rapid walk." Confederate horse artillery opened on the enemy horsemen as they approached in the drizzling rain. Stuart knew the Union VI Corps was behind Buford and called for infantry support. Some of Longstreet's First Corps occupied the region, so Brig. Gen. George Anderson's brigade (now under Col. W. W. White) was sent to help. White was a reluctant savior, arguing with Stuart that he was not under the cavalryman's command and not subject to his orders. After a confrontation, the infantry brigade commander finally relented and reported to Fitz Lee.

Fitz Lee had no clue about commanding a large infantry unit, and he ordered it through Funkstown in a manner that maximized its losses from Union artillery. He compounded the error by deploying the unit too close to the enemy line, resulting in additional casualties. White's infantry and Stuart's cavalry were up against Buford's outnumbered cavalry division. However, the VI Corps arrived and hovered in the rear, perplexing Buford, who rode over to the commander of the first division, Brig. Gen. Albion Howe, to request help. Howe sought permission to move forward to assist the cavalry, but corps commander John Sedgwick waved off the request. Buford persisted, and Howe asked again; this time, Sedgwick gave permission. Colonel Lewis Grant's tough First Vermont Brigade moved forward into position to take on the Confederates. With infantry in place, Buford could follow previous orders to move right, blocking the road leading to Hagerstown.

White's Georgians slugged it out against the Green Mountain boys, but got the worst of it. Stuart quickly responded by throwing another infantry brigade, Col. Goode Bryan's, into the fray, and then repositioned his cavalry to face Buford in his new position. Meanwhile, Bryan attempted to outflank the Vermont boys, but Grant saw the move and quickly responded to neutralize the threat. The fighting continued until nightfall, when Stuart repositioned his men, ending the battle of Funkstown.

JONES' CROSSROADS

THIS CROSSING SERVED DURING JULY 10-15, 1863, AS AN ANCHOR FOR THE FLANKS OF SUCH GATHERING FEDERAL FORCES AS THE RESERVE ARTILLERY AND THE SECOND, THIRD AND TWELFTH CORPS. MINOR SKIRMISHES WITH ELEMENTS OF LEE'S BESIEGED ARMY OF NORTHERN VIRGINIA OCCURRED HERE.

MARYLAND HISTORICAL TRUST
MARYLAND STATE HIGHWAY ADMINISTRATION

$\mathcal{S}$*talemate*

CHAPTER NINE
JULY 11, 1863

Lee continued moving troops into his now-completed defensive works on the morning of July 11. Longstreet's two divisions marched toward Downsville on the Hagerstown-Downsville Road and formed Lee's right flank. John Hood's division formed the army's extreme right, with its right flank extending almost to the Potomac; Lafayette McLaws's division formed on Hood's left. A.P. Hill's Third Corps held the center of Lee's line. Richard Anderson's division connected with McLaws's left flank, and then came Henry Heth's and Dorsey Pender's (now under James Pettigrew) divisions. Ewell's Second Corps held Lee's left flank. Edward Johnson's division's right flank attached itself to Pender's left, and then came Jubal Early's division, and finally Robert Rodes's division, which anchored Lee's left flank to just west of Hagerstown. Lee concentrated cannon between McLaws's and Anderson's divisions as he worried about an attack against his right flank, thinking Meade might attempt to get between him and the river. Lee's left flank held another concentration of artillery.

Jones' Crossroads was well within the Union lines as Meade confronted Lee near Hagerstown. (lg)

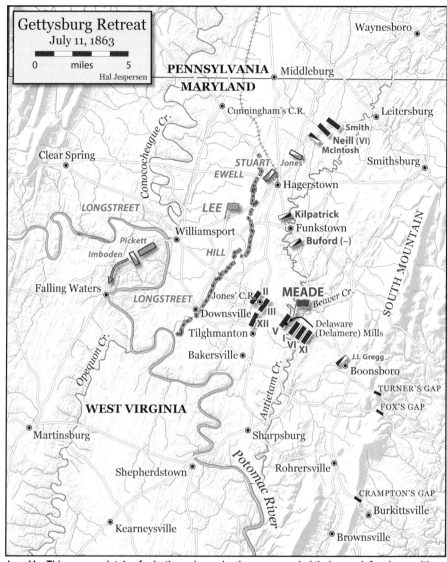

Gettysburg Retreat
July 11, 1863

0   miles   5
Hal Jespersen

JULY 11—This was a quiet day for both armies as Lee's men occupied their new defensive positions and Meade made minor adjustments to his line. Lee's quartermasters continued plying their trade and collected tons of materials from the countryside.

Upon manning the nine-mile-long works, the infantry and artillerymen continued improving their positions under the hot July sun.

The Confederate works were comprised of two parallel lines. The first occupied the forward slope of Salisbury Ridge and was weak compared with the second line. Lee placed his forward skirmish line here. It was not expected to hold for an extended period, but to provide enough time for the men in the second line to prepare for action. This forward line was dug into the ground and then lined with wheat sheaths covered with packed earth to provide additional protection. The second, or main line, was dug below the brow of the ridge and used rocks, fence rails, and packed earth in its construction. The men also dug long ditches in front of the works to delay the enemy's advance.

Lee's defensive line had interior lines, so he benefited from a road network that could quickly shuttle troops from one end of the line to the other. The Union I Corps artillery commander, Col. Charles Wainwright, later walked along the works and called them "by far the strongest I have seen yet; evidently laid out by engineers and built as if they meant to stand a month's siege." Adding to Lee's advantages, torrential rains had turned Marsh Run into a raging stream, forcing the Yankees to wade across waist-high water and then march toward the enemy's line in open and waterlogged terrain that sucked at their shoes and retarded their movements. Historian Kent Masterson Brown opined, "No position ever held by Lee's army, save for Marye's Heights at Fredericksburg, was more formidable." This may be a bit of an exaggeration, as Lee's defensive lines at Mine Run and Petersburg were equally strong.

Lee spent considerable time designing his defensive works, which Union soldiers later called formidable. (loc)

July 11 was a lucrative day for Lee's quartermasters as they continued scouring the environs for livestock, food, and supplies. They seized thousands of pounds of grains and scores of horses and mules. Word of Vicksburg's fall reached the army, causing men to worry even more about the fate of the Confederacy. Wagons arriving on the Virginia side of the river continued delivering supplies and ammunition to Lee's army via the still-operating ferries.

The Army of Northern Virginia was on the verge of fighting for its very life, so Lee issued General Order 76 and instructed its reading to every regiment:

> *After long and trying marches, endured with the fortitude that has ever characterized the soldiers of the Army of Northern Virginia, you have penetrated the country of our enemies, and recalled to the defense of their own soil those who were engaged in the invasion of ours. You have fought a fierce and sanguinary*

Brigadier General William "Baldy" Smith had a distinguished military career up to Antietam. He was demoted for insubordination after the battle of Fredericksburg and sought redemption as a division commander in the Department of the Susquehanna. (loc)

battle, which, if not attended with the success that has hitherto crowned your efforts, was marked by the same heroic spirit that has commanded the respect of your enemies, the gratitude of your country, and the admiration of mankind. Once more you are called upon to meet the army from which you have won on so many fields a name that will never die. Once more the eyes of your countrymen are turned upon you, and again do wives and sisters, fathers, mothers, and helpless children lean for defense on your strong arms and brave hearts. Let every soldier remember that on his courage and fidelity depends all that makes life worth having—the freedom of his country, the honor of his people, and the security of his home. . . .

Despite setbacks, Lee's army remained confident, hoping the Federals would test its new defensive line. However, with Smith's division and Neill's brigade pressing down on his left flank, and Kelley's men marching from western Virginia, Lee relied on Jeb Stuart's cavalry to help protect those sectors. Lee informed Stuart a force of the enemy "may attempt to attack Williamsport on our left." Being approached by strong Union forces on at least three sides shook Lee. Porter Alexander recalled that he "never before, and never afterward saw him as I thought visibly anxious over an approaching action; but I did on this occasion." Lee later admitted he was relieved when Meade manifested "no disposition to attack."

Although many Confederate soldiers realized retreating into Virginia without a fight was an admission of defeat, most had seen enough of Pennsylvania and Maryland. Col. David Aiken of the 7th South Carolina wrote home, "I am sick of Maryland and never want to come [to] this side of the river again . . . we have found a great difference between invading the North & defending the South." Some, like corps commander Richard Ewell, believed his men's "spirit was never better than at this time, and the wish was universal that the enemy would attack" his strong position.

Meade's Army Is Now in Position

Lincoln and Halleck anxiously awaited news of an attack. The President wrote to D. K. Dubois on July 11,

"I am more than satisfied with what has happened north of the Potomac so far, and am anxious and hopeful for what is to come." This optimism would soon be dashed.

Meade has been criticized for not attacking Lee before his army occupied its strong earthworks. Some authors have postulated had Meade "moved more aggressively on July 10 he could have intercepted Lee's men while they were moving into their new line of entrenchments. . . ." They also noted Meade's "inaction was an obvious misreading of, or lack of reaction to, intelligence indicating Lee's army had not yet taken up its new position." Others suggested that "Meade's decision to entrench while still some distance from the ANV [Lee's Army of Northern Virginia] actually boosted the spirits of the demoralized Virginia army. . . ." Even one of Meade's staunchest supporters agreed that he "cautiously advanced his army. . . ."

Lieutenant Elisha Rhodes rose through the ranks from private to colonel of his 2nd Rhode Island Infantry. He sought his mother's permission to enlist in 1861, although he was 19 years old. (loc)

However, in fairness to Meade, his orders from Washington were clear: "advance cautiously . . . postpone a general battle till you can concentrate all your forces and get up your reserves and re-enforcements." Union artilleryman Charles Wainwright summed up the situation best:

If he [Lee] does not clear out soon, we shall have another fight. It would nearly end the rebellion if we could actually bag this army, but, on the other hand, a severe repulse of us would give them all the prestige at home and abroad which they lost at Gettysburg, and injure our morale greatly. I trust, therefore, that Meade will not attempt it, unless under the circumstances which will make our chances of success at least four out of five.

Infantrymen in the ranks also echoed this sentiment. Lieutenant Elisha Rhodes of the 2nd Rhode Island (VI Corps) wrote, "Our Army is very tired and ragged, but we know that if we can destroy Lee's Army now the war is over. This keeps us up to our work."

A commissary sergeant in the 126th Ohio wrote home after the campaign, "It looks as if somebody did not care about having this war finished very

One-armed Maj. Gen. Oliver Howard assumed command of the Union XI Corps prior to the battle of Chancellorsville. His command was defeated during that battle and again at Gettysburg, but the "Christian General" retained command of the corps when it was sent west to fight with William Sherman's army. (loc)

soon." Another wrote that "great dissatisfaction exists among the troops. We were all aware that we only needed the word to advance in order to have scattered the remains of Lee's army to the winds." He added, the "army has got so used to bungles that it almost seems a matter of course."

A New Yorker recognized Meade's efforts at Gettysburg, calling them "first rate." But his views changed during the retreat, concluding, it is "just as I expected . . . Meade was very afraid of a little rain and laid over 24 hours too long and they slipped away." A Bay State soldier angrily recalled, "our army did not want to go back into Virginia to engage in another series of unsuccessful campaigns . . . our commanding officers were condemned in harsh and bitter terms by the rank and file, when it was learned that Lee had crossed the river." Another Massachusetts soldier recalled that all that "seemed necessary was an assault to compel [Lee's] vanquished and retreating army to surrender." He noted how some of the troops cried over the lost opportunity as "one grand, final conflict which might end the whole war, and release them from the privations and sufferings of another campaign in Virginia."

Other soldiers were willing to give Meade the benefit of the doubt. An officer wrote home that newspapers were partly to blame for the army's discontent as they provided "very exaggerated accounts of the effect of the late battle on the Rebel army" that made "great promises of its entire annihilation." He concluded the Army of the Potomac did not have the strength to "give the rebels a blow which will go far to end the war."

Meade made minor adjustments to his position on July 11. The II Corps marched two miles from Tilghmanton to Jones's Crossroads, where its men skirmished with the enemy. During the afternoon, William Hays' II Corps was ordered to send a brigade toward Funkstown to reconnoiter "until it finds the enemy in superior force." The III Corps made modest changes in its position, and was ordered to "mass it in the rear of the V Corps." The V Corps "[m]aneuvered in face of the enemy; constructed breastwork, rifle-pits, &c." and the XII Corps moved north from Bakersville to Fairplay, where it could straddle Jones' Crossroads.

The VI Corps was ordered to send a brigade to occupy Funkstown, which it did. The other corps held their positions. An 88th Pennsylvania (I Corps) officer reported he lay "all day behind breastworks." Most of the corps were ordered to throw out skirmish lines to "feel the enemy."

Reinforcements began reaching Meade's army, leading Oliver Howard to complain, "I think mine now is the only corps that has not been strengthened." Neill's independent command, composed of his brigade and McIntosh's cavalry brigade, was dissolved, and the infantry was ordered back to the VI Corps, taking "inner and circuitous roads" to "avoid the enemy in superior force." Smith's large division was already in Maryland, very close to Hagerstown. Couch expressed concerns to Smith about his men's fitness for action: "I dread the effect on the Army of the Potomac, if our men should conclude not to fight in Maryland or break on the field; I think, however, that a good many of the Pennsylvania troops would do well."

Lee's Pontoon Bridge

CHAPTER TEN

JULY 12, 1863

Lee's troops, now settled into defensive works, continued their strengthening. Stuart's cavalry was sent to the army's left flank beyond Hagerstown with orders to protect the army's vulnerable flank as Smith's division approached from the north. This was not an easy task, given the utter exhaustion of the men and horses after their ordeal that began the second week of June and continued through the retreat. Stuart formed his men in "heavy outposts" from the National Road to Conococheague Creek, a distance of five and a half miles.

Meade Ponders His Options

Just before midnight on July 11, Darius Couch informed Meade that the Confederates had vacated Hagerstown. Meade ordered Howard to send one of his XI Corps brigades to reconnoiter in that direction in conjunction with Kilpatrick's cavalry. Howard reported that Hagerstown was devoid of enemy troops, and his infantry and Kilpatrick's cavalry were

Meade held another council of war at his headquarters near what is now Devil's Backbone State Park. It could have been in this house or one nearby.
(lg)

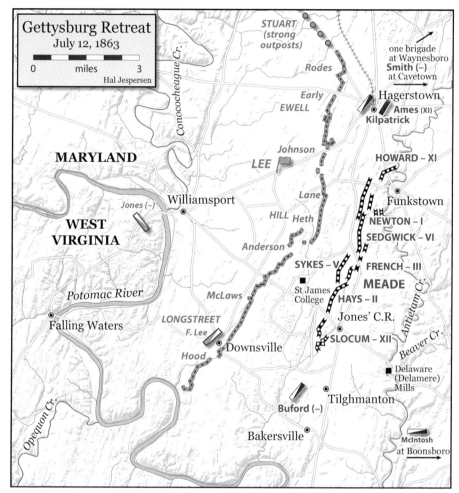

JULY 12—Lee's engineers expedited their work on constructing a pontoon bridge at Falling Waters as the Potomac River began falling after the ongoing torrential rains. Meade made final preparations for his attack on Lee's position from his headquarters at "Devil's Backbone." His senior officers showed little enthusiasm in attacking Lee's army.

occupying the town. John Buford's cavalry division was at the opposite end of the line, scouting Lee's right flank, where he found Longstreet's corps in position. Buford observed rugged terrain and numerous stone walls and pronounced, "The country . . . next to the river is impracticable for any considerable force to advance." Some of his men approached Williamsport and observed the activities along the Potomac River. "Nothing but sick and wounded go over," Buford reported. "At Williamsport there is but one flat-boat, which crosses the river in about seven minutes. It crosses by means of a wire rope. The river is not fordable." General Couch's scouts reported seeing numbers of horses swimming across and noted that 14 flat boats were almost completed.

The final Union position took shape. Meade ordered the XI and I Corps north to occupy Funkstown and the heights beyond. The latter's left flank was fastened to the right of the VI Corps. The line continued south with the V Corps, II Corps, and finally, the XII Corps forming Meade's left flank at Jones' Crossroads. Hays felt he needed reinforcements for his II Corps, so Gen. French of the III Corps, stationed behind him, moved up 2,500 men and another brigade of about 3,000 to form directly in his rear. The remainder of French's corps rested about a mile behind. French worried about the II Corps' poor position "at the base of a sloping ridge." However, he believed if Hays pulled his corps back to a better position, the V Corps on its left would also be required to move to maintain its connection. Meade later ordered Hays back to occupy the crest of the ridge. The V Corps was also on the move, inadvertently creating a void with the II Corps, so Gen. Sykes called upon the III Corps in reserve to help fill it. General Andrew Humphreys, Meade's new chief of staff, immediately voiced his disapproval as it would require 3,000 men and reduce the III Corps, in reserve, "to nil." He instead told Sykes to thin his line and connect his left with the right of the II Corps "in accordance with the instructions this morning."

Other issues arose as the army prepared to take its final positions. Quartermaster Rufus Ingalls informed Meade's staff that cavalry and artillery officers were taking private property without proper payment. "Citizens are calling on me daily, and presenting papers for property taken, but on which no disbursing officer could make payment." He requested orders against this thievery, and Meade complied by creating and distributing the following circular:

[No] private property can be taken for the use of this army as far as relates to the quartermaster's department, excepting by an officer of that department, and he must have the authority of his commanding officer for taking it. Payment must be made at the time, or properly certified accounts given, on Form No. 13,

Brigadier General Andrew Humphreys was one of Meade's most educated lieutenants as he graduated from what is now Moravian College before attending West Point. He served as an infantry division commander at Gettysburg and agreed to serve as Meade's chief of staff after the battle. (loc)

After graduating from West Point, Brig. Gen. Rufus Ingalls served several stints as quartermaster. Because of his strong organizational skills he served as the chief quartermaster of the Army of the Potomac. (loc)

Lieutenant Ranald MacKenzie was an able engineer before and during the Gettysburg Campaign. He later left the engineering corps to join the infantry, rising to the rank of brigadier general and commanding a cavalry division in the Army of the James. (loc)

and the property must be accounted for on the returns of the officer signing the certificate. The accounts must also be approved by the commanding officer.

In testimony before a Congressional hearing after the campaign, Meade claimed he intended to "move the army forward and feel the enemy, and to attack them at such points as he should find it best to attack." Perhaps with that idea in mind, Meade issued a circular to his army at 10:20 a.m.: Chief Engineer Gouverneur Warren would examine the army's position and make changes as necessary. Meade informed the corps commanders at 3:15 p.m. they were "hereby directed to advance their line of pickets until the pickets of the enemy are encountered, and report the character of the country in front."

Meade received an ominous note from Lt. Ranald Mackenzie of the engineers on the afternoon of July 12:

> *The river has fallen here 18 inches in the last twenty-four hours, and is still falling. A citizen states that he is acquainted with the river above here, and that he judges from its appearance at this place that the fords near Shepherdstown and Williamsport are now practicable for infantry.*

At 4:30 p.m., Meade sent a fairly accurate assessment of the Rebel positions to Halleck, explaining they ran "along the high ground from Downsville to near Hagerstown. This position they are intrenching. Batteries are established on it." He then made a statement that would come back to haunt him and reduce his stature in the eyes of Lincoln and Halleck:

> *It is my intention to attack them to-morrow, unless something intervenes to prevent it, for the reason that delay will strengthen the enemy and will not increase my force.*

During an extensive examination of the Army of Northern Virginia's defensive line, Andrew Humphreys noted, "Wherever seen the [enemy] position was naturally strong, and was strongly intrenched; it presented no vulnerable points, but much of it was concealed from view." Meade began having second thoughts about an attack on the enemy's strong positions. He later explained that a defeat would cause "the road to Washington and to the north [to be] open, and all the fruits of my victory at Gettysburg dissipated." Meade also learned that Lee's army had been resupplied with ammunition and remained dangerous. He took some time to pen a letter to his wife, informing her that he and his son, an aide, were well, that the enemy was entrenching, and that "I shall be patient & not act rashly."

Major General George Sykes was a career army officer who rose to command the Union V Corps after George Meade assumed leadership of the Army of the Potomac. Sykes suffered from severe sciatica and, by the spring of 1864, assumed a less-strenuous role as commander of the Department of Kansas. (loc)

Meade had moved his headquarters to what is now called "Devil's Backbone" along the Boonsboro-Williamsport Road, where it crossed Antietam Creek. He confided to his wife that he suffered "much from anxiety and responsibility. . . . I am trying to do the best I can, leaving it to Providence to shape & direct my fate." The inexperienced army commander turned to his senior lieutenants once again for advice, calling a council of war at 8:00 p.m. that night. Most present were seasoned corps commanders, such as George Sykes (V Corps), John Sedgwick (VI Corps), Oliver Howard (XI Corps), and Henry Slocum (XII Corps). Three present had never commanded a corps in battle: because John Newton (I Corps) was ill, division commander, James Wadsworth, represented him. William Hays (II Corps) and William French (III Corps) were also novices. Also present were Meade's new chief of staff, Brig. Gen. Andrew Humphreys, Cavalry chief Alfred Pleasonton and chief engineer, Gouverneur Warren.

Meade began the meeting by recounting four major points:

1. "General Lee's position was a very strong one, and that he was prepared to give battle and defend it if attacked."

2. Meade could not determine the "precise point of attack . . ." because of a lack of time and proper reconnaissance.

3. But Meade claimed, "nevertheless, I was in favor of moving forward and attacking the enemy and taking the consequences."

4. Ultimately, Meade "left it to their judgement, and would not do it unless it met with their approval."

Meade later reported the group "was very largely opposed to any attack without further examination." All but Wadsworth, Howard, and Pleasonton expressed reservations. "I yielded, or abstained from ordering an assault," explained Meade, and instead settled on more thorough "examinations of the enemy's position as would enable us to form some judgment as to where he might be attacked with some degree and probability of success." French purportedly told Meade at the meeting, "Why it does not make any difference what our opinions are; if you give the order to attack, we will fight just as well under it as if our opinions were not against it."

Lee's Pontoon Bridge Takes Shape

Hour by hour, Meade's opportunity to attack the Army of Northern Virginia slipped through his fingers as Lee's pontoon bridge took shape. Captain Summerfield Smith's engineer battalion left Hagerstown at 5:00 a.m. on July 10 and traveled eight miles to Williamsport. With the army's entrenchments completed, the pioneer company of each division was detached and sent to Williamsport to aid in the bridge-building effort. Officers immediately drafted plans for the bridge as enlisted men scoured the area for suitable wood. They found 16 pontoons that spanned the river before being destroyed by enemy cavalry on July 4, determining ten of them could be repaired. The men constructed 16 additional pontoons using materials found at local sawmills. They also dismantled barns and warehouses for wood. Each pontoon measured 30 feet long at the top, then curved to only 18 feet below the surface. The bottom of the boats were liberally smeared with hot tar for waterproofing. After being built at Williamsport, the pontoon boats were floated downstream to Falling Waters, where they were secured to other pontoons. Other engineers worked on approaches and exits to the bridge.

The first pontoon was pushed into the Potomac River at 9:00 a.m. on July 12 and took about two and a half hours to float downstream, more than six miles to Falling Waters. The men worked around the clock to build pontoons, connect trestles, and float them downriver. The completed bridge spanned 800 feet, and by 11:00 p.m. on July 12, Lee ordered all wagons still at Williamsport to begin making their way south to Falling Waters via the canal towpath. It took 26 hours for the wagons to cross. Cavalry also crossed the river to protect wagons as they traveled south in Virginia. Heavy rains again soaked the region, making travel to the bridges difficult. The engineers also created a defensive line more than a mile from the bridge to hold back an enemy attack while Lee's troops made their way to safety. As the bridge reached completion, Lee received word the river had fallen and would only be four feet deep by the morning of July 13.

Lee never intended to halt his command on the Maryland side of the Potomac to give battle to Meade. He wrote to his wife on July 12, "[h]ad the late unexpected rise [of the Potomac River] not occurred, there would have been no cause for anxiety, as it would have been in my power to recross the Potomac on my first reaching it without molestation." As it turned out, both army commanders were against fighting another battle so soon: Lee because his back was against the river, and he knew he was heavily outnumbered; Meade because he worried about defeat and squandering his victory at Gettysburg. Of the two, Meade was most likely to launch the offensive, but as Lt. Col. Walter Taylor of Lee's staff noted, the Confederate army was in position and "ready and anxious for attack . . . but steadily engaged in throwing up earthworks for defense."

Walter Taylor (right) served through the war as one of Robert E. Lee's top aides. He became a banker and attorney after the war and died in 1916. (loc)

Lee anticipated an attack on his position on July 13 between the Williamsport-Boonsboro Road and the National Pike, where Meade seemed to have concentrated many of his troops. Lee was also concerned about the disparity in the length of his line (10 miles) in relation to Meade's (five miles long). The flanks of both armies essentially hung in the air. Meade's right flank was anchored on Antietam Creek, but his left was vulnerable. Lee's left flank was also weak, and both army commanders ordered this cavalry to protect those flanks.

Planning and Vacillating

CHAPTER ELEVEN
JULY 13, 1863

During the rainy morning of July 13, the Union army continued adjusting its lines in case Meade decided to attack. Meade spent considerable time riding along the lines, peering intently at Lee's defensive line. At 5:00 p.m., Meade sent a message to Halleck that triggered several highly disappointing communications. He noted his intention to "attack the enemy today, unless something intervenes to prevent it." However, he then continued with a slight exaggeration: "[u]pon calling my corps commanders together and submitting the question to them, five out of six were unqualifiedly opposed to it," and noted, "[u]nder these circumstances, in view of the momentous consequences attendant upon a failure to succeed, I did not feel myself authorized to attack until after I had made more careful examination of the enemy's position, strength, and defensive works." These reconnaissances were underway, showing the "enemy to be strongly intrenched on a ridge running from the rear of Hagerstown past Downsville to the Potomac." Meade hoped to find "some weak point" in

The name of Falling Waters, West Virginia, comes from the small waterfall nearby. (lg)

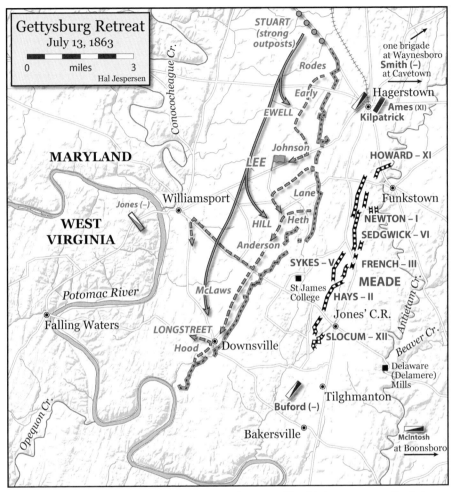

JULY 13—With his pontoon bridge completed, Lee began pushing his troops across the Potomac River. Meade remained in planning mode, sending out orders for several reconnaissances the following day.

Lee's defensive line before "I shall hazard an attack." He also informed Halleck that Smith's division had arrived but was dismayed by its "organization and condition" and concluded "I cannot place much reliance upon them." Meade's chief quartermaster noted the men's "destitute condition."

Halleck did not respond for several hours. The tenor and tone of the resulting 9:30 p.m. telegram reflected his unhappiness with Meade about his continued reluctance in attacking and relying too much on his subordinates for advice: "You are strong enough to attack and defeat the enemy before he can effect a crossing. Act upon your own judgment and make your generals execute your orders. Call no council of war. It is proverbial that councils of war never fight. Re-enforcements are pushed on as rapidly as possible. Do not let the enemy escape."

Around this time, Halleck wrote to Gen. Kelley, whose men were slogging slowly through western Maryland toward Lee's army, telling him to "Move up upon the enemy's flank and rear, and attack and harass him wherever you can. If you can reach his crossing, annoy him as much as possible."

At about the same time Halleck was drafting his response, Meade was completing his own orders for his troops for July 14. Each corps commander sent out a reconnaissance in force at 7:00 a.m., consisting of at least a division, commanded by a general officer. Each officer was to report on the "position of the enemy, the arrangement of his troops, the number, strength, and position of his batteries, rifle-pits, and other defensive works." They were to "hold their troops under arms in readiness for a general engagement, should the enemy offer one in front of his line of supposed intrenchments." It appears clear Meade did not intend to attack on July 14.

Reinforcements continued to reach Meade's army. Individual regiments were quickly incorporated into veteran units. Smith's division reached Hagerstown, and another one of Couch's divisions, composed of 7,000 men, awaited a call from Meade, which never came. Perhaps he worried about the preparedness and helpfulness of the militia and National Guard units.

Brigadier General Benjamin Kelly was a freight agent for the B&O Railroad prior to the Civil War, but quickly rose to the rank of brigadier general. By Gettysburg, he commanded the Department of West Virginia. (loc)

Lee Prepares to Send His Army Across the Potomac River

Lee spent much of July 13 planning his army's evacuation from Maryland. He requested a visit from Imboden, and the cavalry brigade commander rode over to meet Lee at the northern part of the defensive line. Lee believed Imboden knew the fords across the Potomac River and asked him to "name and describe ford after ford all the way up to Cumberland [Maryland], and to describe minutely their character, and the roads and surrounding country on both sides of the river," according to the cavalry commander. After receiving his information, Lee requested the

The march down Falling Waters Road brought the Confederate First and Third Corps to the pontoon bridge near Falling Waters. The road is now on private property and is inaccessible. (lg)

services of Imboden's brother and his 18th Virginia Cavalry to screen the troop movements to the ford. Imboden recalled how heavily the army's safety weighed on Lee's shoulders. As Imboden was about to leave, Lee asked, with a twinkle in his eye, if it "ever quits raining about here. If so, I should like to see a clear day soon."

To prepare for the crossing, Lee sent Grumble Jones's brigade across the river to patrol the road leading to Winchester. At about 5:00 p.m., Lee ordered his commanders to prepare to vacate their defensive lines and head for the river. As darkness and heavy rains enveloped the area, Lee began implementing his plan. Ewell's men would march about six miles to Williamsport and ford the river, while Longstreet's and Hill's men crossed over the now-completed 800-foot pontoon bridge at Falling Waters. All the remaining wagons and wounded who could be safely

moved (about 200 of the badly wounded were left behind) joined the column to the bridge. Lee charged his cavalry with occupying the lines, and holding back any enemy pursuit until the last of the army had successfully crossed. Stuart was told to be "very vigilant and bold, and not let the enemy discover that our lines have been vacated." Stuart's men would then cross the river and protect Lee's rear with part of his division while others screened the front of the army.

Even with their departure imminent, Lee's quartermasters continued scouring the countryside for supplies. One artillery battalion seized 18,500 pounds of hay and 25 horses on July 13.

Most of the Confederate army crossed the Potomac River on the night of July 13-14. Although fires illuminated the path, accidents occasionally occurred. (cm)

Meade's Bridge-Building Activities

There is little to suggest Meade made constructing bridges a priority or considered any attempts to disrupt Lee's bridge-building activities. Meade did order them from Washington to Harpers Ferry on July 9. On July 13, Meade's chief engineer sent a message to the officer in charge of building the pontoon bridge, "We may want a bridge put across the river before long." Col. Ira Spaulding responded the following day by predicting it could be completed by 2:00 p.m. By July 14, two bridges snaked across the Potomac River at Berlin, Maryland (now Brunswick) and another at Sandy Hook to the north.

Lee's Crossing

CHAPTER TWELVE
JULY 14, 1863

At Falling Waters, the defensive positions of Brig. Gen. Joseph Davis's and Col. John Brockenbrough's brigades were across the road from what is now the protected portion of the battlefield. Unfortunately, landowners who do not support battlefield preservation own key portions of the field. (lg)

Lee's men slowly crossed the Potomac River on the night of July 13-14. Each brigade left one regiment to cover the defensive line until the rest of the unit was well toward the river. Blackened logs were placed into position to deceive the enemy into thinking they were cannons, and campfires blazed along the line. Rain continued falling, causing an artilleryman to recall the "blackness of the night was phenomenal." Well-spaced torches lit the road. The roads again became quagmires, causing many wagons to become bogged in the mud. Longstreet's men marched along the Hagerstown-Downsville Road and Falling Waters Road to reach the bridge after dark. A soldier in the 3rd South Carolina (McLaws's division) claimed the night was the "worse [he] ever saw." The mud "was almost knee deep and about as thick as corn meal batter. We waded through it like horses, and such squashing you never heard. I believe I had over fifteen or twenty pounds of mud clinging to my shoes and pants." According to a Virginian, men were "falling down continually, sometimes head and ears in

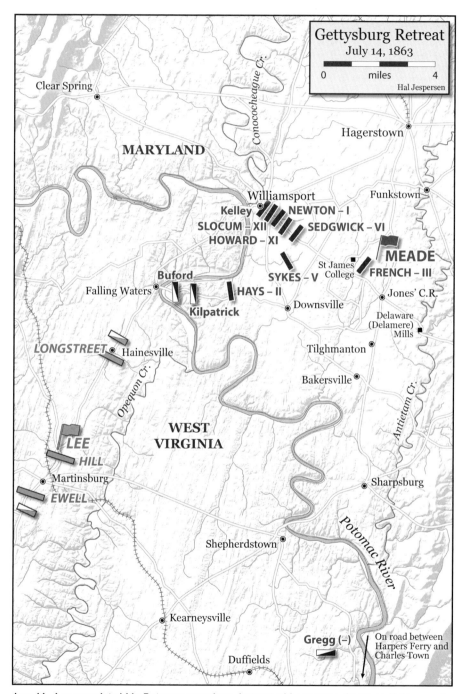

JULY **14**—Lee completed his Potomac crossings, but not without some drama as Union cavalry attacked the Confederate rearguard across the river from Falling Waters, capturing hundreds of troops and mortally wounding Brig. Gen. James Pettigrew.

This sketch by Edwin Forbes shows Lee's infantry and wagons crossing the Potomac River on a pontoon bridge. (loc)

mud and water, losing their muskets, sometimes five minutes would elapse before they could be recovered in the darkness."

Ewell's men began wading across the river at fords around Williamsport at about midnight and found the water very cold and deep—up to the men's armpits or higher, which slowed the march. Bonfires on either bank helped illuminate the passage. Men held ammunition high over their heads, although thousands of rounds were drenched and unusable. Robert Rodes's division crossed first, followed by Edward Johnson's and then Jubal Early's. Shouting and jokes punctuated the crossing. One soldier shouted to a shorter one, "Run here, little boy, and get on my back, and I'll carry you over safely!" Another quipped that it was their first bath in months, and "General Lee knows we need it!" The entire corps was across the river by 8:00 a.m. on July 14. Ewell knew his artillery could not ford the still-high river, so he depended on the ferryboats, but "when it was time for them to cross, none were to be found, nor [was] any one in charge; it was dark and raining. . . . Everything was in confusion." Ewell decided to send them down to Falling Waters to cross at the bridge.

An uncharacteristically anxious Lee crossed the river on the bridge and positioned himself on the southern shore, watching the slow progress.

Because of the slow passage of wagons, artillery, and Longstreet's corps over the bridge at Falling Waters, Hill's Third Corps did not begin crossing until after sunrise. Lee withdrew his two flanks first

Major General Henry "Harry" Heth graduated at the bottom of his 1847 West Point class. Purportedly the only subordinate whom Lee addressed by his first name, Heth missed most of the battle of Gettysburg after being knocked unconscious by a piece of shell. (loc)

and left Hill's Corps in the center to cover their passage. Richard Anderson's division finally led the corps across the bridge. Dorsey Pender's (under James Pettigrew) followed as Harry Heth's division formed the rearguard. A. P. Hill ordered Heth to position his troops on either side of the road leading to the bridge as a protective rearguard. Heth requested artillery support, but Hill rejected it. Although not part of the rearguard, Pender's division waited until the bridge cleared and formed about 200 yards behind Heth's men. Fitz Lee's cavalry brigade hovered nearby, so Heth allowed his men to rest after stacking their arms without throwing out a picket line. Gen. Pettigrew thought Heth was rash, so he took it upon himself to send out soldiers to screen the front of the defensive line. None could know danger was galloping toward them in the pouring rain.

The Battle at Falling Waters

Judson Kilpatrick's men were awakened in their camps south of Hagerstown at 3:00 a.m. and ordered to ride toward Williamsport at 7:00 a.m. The downpour ceased, but a heavy fog ensued. George Custer and his Wolverine cavalry brigade took the lead, but quickly realized the enemy had evacuated its works between Hagerstown and Williamsport. The division then headed toward the latter town, hoping to find some

Edwin Forbes's sketch of the fight at Falling Waters captures the initial confusion of Henry Heth's men when attacked by members of the 6th Michigan. (loc)

of Lee's men still in the area. However, upon arriving at Williamsport, they could only see Ewell's Corps on the Virginia side of the river. Confederate stragglers told of a pontoon bridge further south, near Falling Waters, so Custer headed in that direction, led by two companies of the 6th Michigan. The 5th Michigan Cavalry stayed at Williamsport to round up prisoners.

Heth's men faced a mile-long open area, reducing the possibility of a surprise attack by enemy troops. Henry Heth, alerted to some troopers approaching, trained his binoculars on them at around 11:30 a.m. Unable to make out their identity, as mud and grime made all uniforms look the same, he asked Pettigrew if he thought they were Fitz Lee's troopers. Both were incorrect, as Maj. Peter Weber's small contingent from the 6th Michigan Cavalry approached. When he observed the Confederates up ahead, Weber turned to Custer and Kilpatrick for orders. The latter told him to charge the enemy. As the troopers neared, Weber yelled out, "Wheel into line and damn them, split their heads open!" Some Confederate officers ordered their men to open fire, but Heth countermanded the orders.

Brigadier General James Pettigrew may have been the most accomplished and literate member of Lee's general officers. Despite a lack of formal military training, he effectively commanded his troops in battle. His loss was universally mourned by the army. (loc)

Weber's men were soon among the Confederate infantry, yelling, "Surrender!" Heth finally realized his error and ordered his men to open fire, but Weber's men galloped through the Confederate line, "yelling, cutting right and left, and riding over [some of Heth's men] while asleep breaking arms and legs and tramping some to death." Confederate officers assembled something like a line of battle, supported by the now-alerted men of Pender's division. Seeing his front closing, Weber ordered his men to turn and again attack Heth's men. Weber and most of his men were killed or wounded, but they did grave damage.

General Pettigrew observed a lone Union trooper behind a barn, and when his men were unable to bring him down, he pulled out his own revolver and headed in that direction. The trooper fired first, sending the round ripping into Pettigrew's abdomen. One of Pettigrew's men then ran over and killed the Michigander. Confederate surgeons believed Pettigrew's only hope was to be left behind and not moved, but the general declared, "I would die before I would again be taken a prisoner." He did so three days later.

Major General J. E. B. Stuart's cavalry reached the Virginia side of the Potomac River with a wealth of horses. Both sides often suffered from an inadequate number of horses. (loc)

Hundreds of other Confederate infantrymen were killed, missing, or captured as Kilpatrick brought up additional troops, supported by an ever-growing assemblage of artillery. Buford's cavalry division also arrived and pitched into the fight. Heth's men extricated themselves and crossed the river. The 26th North Carolina was the last unit across. The regiment had lost more than 80% of its men at Gettysburg. The pontoon bridge was quickly disassembled when it finished its crossing.

Meade Must Inform Washington of the News

Meade received horrible news from Gen. Howard prior to 7:00 a.m.: "My brigade commander in Hagerstown reports the works in his front evacuated." Howard sent another dispatch at 8:00 a.m.: "Enemy's works very strong. [The enemy] [c]ommenced moving at dusk: last left about midnight." Meade realized Lee's army had plenty of time to cross the river before he was made aware of it. Other reconnaissances also found the enemy's works abandoned. Meade immediately ordered a pursuit, but not before his troops roamed about abandoned works, marveling over their strength and surmising an attack could have led to a bloody repulse. Many of Meade's men were nevertheless furious when they learned of Lee's retreat across the Potomac River.

At 11:00 a.m., Meade drafted a difficult communication to Washington: "On advancing my army this morning, with a view of ascertaining the exact position of the enemy and attacking him if the result of the examination should justify one, I found on reaching his lines, that they were evacuated. I immediately put my army in pursuit, the cavalry in advance."

Halleck responded several hours later: "The enemy should be pursued and cut up, wherever he may have gone." After discussing some logistical issues, he added: "I need hardly say to you that the escape of Lee's army without another battle has created great dissatisfaction in the mind of the President, and it will require an active and energetic pursuit on your part to remove the impression that it has not been sufficiently active heretofore." The communication irked Meade, a sensitive man who had done what other commanders could not—decisively best Lee.

Meade replied to Halleck at 2:30 p.m.: "Having performed my duty conscientiously and to the best of my ability, the censure of the President conveyed in your dispatch of 1 p.m. this day, is, in my judgment, so undeserved that I feel compelled most respectfully to ask to be immediately relieved from the command of this army." To Meade's credit, he continued commanding the army, issuing directives, and communicating with Halleck. The latter, realizing how his words had stung Meade, probably again conferred with Lincoln and at 4:30 p.m. responded: "My telegram, stating the disappointment of the President at the escape of Lee's army, was not intended as a censure, but as a stimulus to an active pursuit. It is not deemed a sufficient cause for your application to be relieved."

Aftermath

The venerable Chesapeake
and Ohio Canal linked
Cumberland, Maryland,
with Washington D.C. The
first section of the 50-mile
canal opened in 1830 and
was completed 20 years
later. It was an impediment
for the Confederate wagons
attempting to reach the
Potomac River. (lg)

Meade ordered his army to his pontoon bridges
on July 15. The I, V, VI, and XI Corps, Kilpatrick's
and Buford's cavalry divisions, and the Reserve
Artillery headed to Berlin; the II, III, and XII Corps,
along with Gregg's cavalry division, were directed to
Sandy Hook. Gregg's cavalry was the first to cross on
July 15. He quickly rode north to Shepherdstown,
West Virginia, where troopers engaged in a series
of fights with Fitz Lee's cavalry brigade on July 16.
William French's III Corps was ordered over the
bridge and into West Virginia at 2:00 p.m. on July 17,
and the remainder of the army continued crossing the
following day. The army then entered the Loudoun
Valley and seized several strategically important passes
in the Blue Ridge Mountains.

Once across the Potomac, Lee's army headed
south on the Valley Turnpike to Martinsburg, West
Virginia. Ewell's men led the march, followed by Hill,
and Longstreet brought up the rear. The men finally

Meade's army finally crossed the Potomac River into Virginia on these two pontoon bridges that were quickly laid by the army's engineers. (loc)

reached Darkesville and Bunker Hill, where they were permitted to rest for several days before continuing up the Shenandoah Valley. The sick and wounded were cared for in Martinsburg and Winchester. Lee's army had lost about 4,700 killed or mortally wounded in the fields of Gettysburg. While Lee brought more than 8,000 wounded back to Virginia, he was forced to leave 6,739 behind.

Unlike Lee's first invasion of the North, the Union Army quickly followed the Confederate Army across the Potomac River. Maneuvering and some fighting occurred for the next few weeks until Lee reached Orange Court House, where he could rest and resupply.

Meade never recovered after learning of Lincoln's profound disappointment. The feeling that Meade was timid in not attacking Lee before he escaped was shared by cabinet members and many political leaders. However, many historians have recently come to Meade's defense. Kent Masterson Brown wrote Meade's "crippled, hungry, and exhausted army was facing the prospects of assaulting Lee's elaborate and virtually impregnable defenses. Meade observed them; Lincoln did not. . . . One wonders, though, what Meade's detractors, including Lincoln . . . would have said had Meade attacked . . . and suffered a bloody and crippling repulse, which likely would have occurred. We will never know."

The sleepy town of Greencastle, Pennsylvania, saw a series of fights as John Imboden's wagons rolled through the town on their way to Williamsport. The photo shows the town square. (lg)

The Wagon Train of Misery Tour

TOUR A

Five driving tours are included in this book that will help you to better understand the terrain and the armies' movements at the conclusion of the battle of Gettysburg.

Brigadier General John Imboden was given explicit orders directly from Robert E. Lee: Get the thousands of wounded soldiers to the safety of Williamsport, Maryland, where fords and a pontoon bridge spanning the Potomac River would allow easy entry into Virginia. Unbeknownst to Lee, Imboden, and everyone else in the Army of Northern Virginia, the bridge was destroyed on July 4, and torrential rains would swell the river to 13 feet deep or more, closing off the fords.

This tour follows the general route of Imboden's wagon train from the environs of Gettysburg to Williamsport.

Starting Point: Herr Tavern on Rt. 30

The tavern has a rich history from its construction in 1815. Thousands of Confederates marched past this venerable landmark on Chambersburg Pike on their way to the Gettysburg battleground.

 ## TO STOP 1

As you drive west on Rt. 30 from Herr Tavern, try to visualize the hundreds of wagons—over 1,000—assembling for Imboden's arduous journey. At about six miles from the Herr Tavern, you will see a blinking light, and make a left turn, and drive about a mile to Cashtown.

Stop 1 – *Cashtown Inn*

The Cashtown Inn was built in 1815 and has served, off and on, as a bed and breakfast establishment. People came to Cashtown before the war because of its "pure mountain air" and natural springs nearby. (lg)

Making a right at the dead end brings you onto the very route (Old Route 30) that the Confederates used before and after the battle. The Inn is located at 1325 Old Rte 30.

This road ascends the Cashtown Pass and empties into the modern Rt. 30.

 **TO STOP 2**

Turn left onto the modern route. At the traffic light (Pine Grove Road—Rt. 233) make a right and pull into the parking lot.

Stop 2 – *Thaddeus Stevens's Caledonia Furnace and Iron Works*

The Confederates destroyed Thaddeus Stevens's Iron Works on June 26, 1863, as they marched on Gettysburg. You can still see the blacksmith shop across Pine Grove Road. This area saw fighting on July 5 between Imboden's rearguard and Gen. David Gregg's pursuing Union cavalry.

The Caledonia Iron Works was owned by abolitionist and congressman, Thaddeus Stevens. Major General Jubal Early's men destroyed most of the complex prior to the battle of Gettysburg, but the blacksmith shop remains. (lg)

To Stop 3

Pull back onto Rt. 30 and continue just over two miles to the intersection with Rt. 997. This intersection is marked by a traffic light.

 Stop 3 — Leaving the Chambersburg Pike

Make a left turn onto Rt. 997 (Anthony Highway). This was not the actual road used by Imboden's wagons—a road named Pine Stump Road closely followed this route. You may see portions of it on the right side of the road.

In about half a mile, make a right turn onto Bikle Road, which again, was not here during the Civil War, but it closely follows the original road. Bikle Road runs into Mont Alto Road. The very small village of Duffield sits at the four-way stop. This community was called "New Guilford" during the Civil War. The roads used in this area were among the oldest in the region. A local citizen noted that the road was in a "most deplorable condition, becoming almost impassible." Residents recalled how the wagon train rumbled past their homes for about 48 hours. They would never forget the horrible condition of the wounded, as their wounds had not been dressed and they were "black and blue" and, in many cases, still oozed body fluids.

➡ TO STOP 4

Cross the intersection and make a quick left onto New Franklin Road.

Stop 4 – The Jeremiah George and Jacob Snyder Homes

Drive about three miles to the location of the Jeremiah George farm. None of the buildings still exist, but a number of the wagons stopped here and at the Jacob Snyder home, just down the road (on the right). Many wounded left the wagon train to beg for shelter, medical attention, and food at these two homes and a number of dead were buried by the side of the road. They may still be reposing here as you drive by.

The Jacob Snyder home (2555 New Franklin Road) is within a third of a mile on this road. The springhouse behind the home (on its left side) supplied the men with

Jacob Snyder's home was along the path of Imboden's wagon train, and therefore, he and his family had a number of interactions with the Confederates. On several occasions, he observed the dead being removed from the wagons and buried along the side of the road. (lg)

water. Many had their wounds dressed here for the first time. Milton Snyder (Jacob Snyder's son) left an account of some of the dead being rapidly buried and the dying men left by the side of the road. Major Donald McLeod of the 8th South Carolina died during the journey, and during a stop by the farm, his slave buried him by the side of the road. The former slave returned to the George farm after the war to help reclaim his former master's body. The nearby railroad was not here in 1863.

 ## To Stop 5

Continue to the intersection with the traffic light, make a left onto Wayne Road (Rt. 316) and drive through New Franklin. Drive 0.1 miles to the Michael Hege farm (on the right).

Stop 5 – The Hege Farm

The farmhouse and barn were built around 1820. Hege's farm was visited by Confederates on their way to Gettysburg, taking $626 worth of livestock and goods, which was quite a bit of money back then. The retreating Confederates again passed his house during their retreat, taking a horse, flour, and meat on July 5.

 ## To Stop 6

Drive about half a mile farther and turn right onto Rt. 914 (Swamp Fox Road). This road dead ends, so make a right onto Marion Road (which is a continuation of Rt. 914). After another couple of miles, turn left onto Rt. 11 (Valley Pike).

Stop 6 – Redirecting Some Wagons to Chambersburg

This is supposed to be where several wagons were intentionally redirected to Chambersburg. The main wagon train turned left; the wayward wagons turned right to Chambersburg. The many period homes lining the road bore witness to the wagon train.

 ## To Stop 7

Continue driving another four and a half miles on Rt. 11 to the Fleming farm, which is on the right side of the road.

Stop 7 – Monument to Corporal William Rihl

Corporal William Rihl had the distinction of being the first soldier killed during Lee's invasion of Pennsylvania. He died on this spot on June 22, 1863. (lg)

You will see an obelisk by the side of the road that pays tribute to Cpl. William Rihl (1st New York Cavalry), who was killed during a skirmish with the 14th Virginia Cavalry on June 22, 1863. He was the first casualty of the Gettysburg Campaign.

 TO STOP 8

Rt. 11 flows through Greencastle. Drive another third of a mile from the Fleming farm and make a left onto Walter Avenue and then an immediate right onto North Carlisle Street.

Stop 8 – Greencastle's Historic Square

You are now approaching Greencastle's historic district. Around this area, Capt. Ulric Dahlgren surprised some Confederate cavalry on July 2, 1863, driving them away and capturing documents informing Lee that he should expect no additional reinforcements.

➤ TO STOP 9

Continue driving south on N. Carlisle Street to the town square (intersection with Baltimore Street).

Stop 9 – Greencastle's Civilians Attack Imboden's Train

Townspeople barricaded the street in this area on July 5, and attacked several of Imboden's wagons. They were ultimately driven away by Confederate cavalry.

➤ TO STOP 10

Continue driving about half a mile from the Square (N. Carlisle Street becomes S. Carlisle Street) and turn right to get back on Rt. 11 (note: this route is not marked here). After only a tenth of a mile, turn left onto Williamsport Pike (Rt. 63). It was called "Greencastle Road" in 1863.

Stop 10 – Attack on Imboden's Wagons

Drive another half a mile to where Imboden's wagons were attacked at dawn on July 5, 1863, by Capt. Ulric Dahlgren and 100 troopers from the 6th Pennsylvania Cavalry. He was joined by 30-40 Greencastle civilians who were organized by Tom Pawling, a resident of Greencastle.

➤ TO STOP 11

After driving another mile and a half, you may see a large red brick Johnston Distillery off to your right.

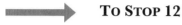

Stop 11 – The Johnson Distillery

Legend has it that several dead were buried along the side of the road here, some of whom were brought home by loved ones after the war.

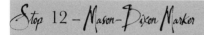 **TO STOP 12**

Drive another two and a half miles and you will cross into Maryland.

Stop 12 – Mason-Dixon Marker

Not many Mason-Dixon markers still exist today. This marker along the side of the road was put in place by the Pennsylvania Department of Highways long after the war. (lg)

You will see a historical marker about the Mason-Dixon Line on the right. If you carefully pull over, you will see an original 1763-67 survey marker in a privately owned field on the left side of the road.

 **TO STOP 13**

Drive another mile and a half to the town of Cearfoss. The town was called "Cunningham's Crossroads" in 1863. At the traffic circle, continue on Rt. 63 (south) and pull into the convenience store parking lot on your right.

Stop 13 – Cearfoss

During the afternoon of July 5, 1863, Imboden's wagons were again attacked in this vicinity by elements of the 1st New York Cavalry and 12th Pennsylvania Cavalry, led by Capt. Abram Jones. If you look several hundred yards to the right of Rt. 63, you will see a white farmhouse on a low bluff. Jones and his men hid behind this hill, before charging into the wagons.

To Stop 14

We are now on our way to Williamsport, Imboden's final destination. Continue on Rt. 63 (south) for just over three and a half miles and as you cross the National Pike (Rt. 40).

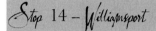

Stop 14 – Williamsport

Look to your left, and you will see a portion of Salisbury Ridge that held the Confederate defensive line skirting Williamsport.

Continue driving south on Rt. 63 and enter Williamsport in just over three and a half miles. Look to your left, and you will see high ground where Imboden anchored the left of his line during his defense of Williamsport on July 6.

After a block, turn right onto Potomac Street, and then after another half a mile, turn right into the C&O parking lot. Park your car, and walk along the canal, which became somewhat of a barrier to the men and wagons under Imboden's care.

Cross the canal on the elevated pedestrian crossing, and walk to the bowl-shaped ground between the canal and the Potomac River. This is where Imboden parked hundreds of wagons, axle to axle, while they were awaiting passage across the river.

Although small, the Monterey
Pass Museum is packed with
useful information on the battle.
(lg)

Monterey Pass

TOUR B

This tour begins in Fairfield, Pennsylvania and initially follows James Longstreet's Corps' march (with his wagons, over 4,000 prisoners, and General Lee, who was traveling with Longstreet) up Jack's Mountain to the Emmitsburg-Waynesboro Pike. As you leave Fairfield, driving south on Rt. 116, the road will fork. Take the right fork—Jack's Mountain Road. You will cross a quaint, one-lane covered bridge spanning Tom's Creek, and then begin your climb up the mountain. Imagine what it must have been like for Longstreet's men and wagons to traverse this windy, steep road. This takes you to the fighting that occurred at Monterey Pass.

Battle at Monterey Pass

The 1st Michigan Cavalry's Route

On the night of July 4, the 1st Michigan was detached from Gen. Judson Kilpatrick's division, marching up the Emmitsburg-Waynesboro Pike toward Monterey Pass, and sent up the Jack's Mountain Road toward you to protect against an attack by Confederates down this road. Probably at the road's highest point, they encountered several units from Gen. William Jones's and Gen. Beverly Robertson's Confederate cavalry brigades guarding the road. After several charges and countercharges, the Confederates were driven back, and the Michiganders constructed a barricade across this road. Several companies of the 1st Michigan were left to guard the road while the rest returned to their regiment.

After several steep and windy miles, you will approach where Jack's Mountain Road dead-ends at Rt. 16, the modern Waynesboro Pike.

Old Waynesboro Pike intersects Jack's Mountain Road about a block before you reach modern Rt. 116. Make a right onto the Old Waynesboro Pike. This was the original Emmitsburg-Waynesboro Pike used by Gen. Judson's Kilpatrick's division riding up the side of South Mountain during the night of July 4-5. The road merges with the modern Rt. 16 and then branches off again after a short distance and travels through the community of Fountaindale, which saw considerable action before and after the Gettysburg Campaign.

1st Michigan's Patrol

You will pass the Fountaindale Fire Department on the left and ascend the steep mountainside. Carefully look to the left, and you will see the steep drop-off that worried many of Kilpatrick's men as they rode up the mountain. As you cross the railroad, Furnace Road is on your right. This portion of Furnace Road did not exist during the battle. The 1st Michigan Cavalry was detached and sent toward Fairfield Gap to intercept wagons further toward Fairfield. They would have used old farm lanes and woods near the present-day Furnace Road to get there. The wagon train, at this point, was well guarded by the Confederates, and the Union troops were repulsed.

This monument to David Miller, the long-time proprietor of the Clermont Hotel near Monterey, is easy to miss as one drives down the road. (lg)

Site of the Initial Fighting

The road will curve as you approach the railroad tracks (not present during the battle). This is believed to be the first location where Capt. George Emack's Marylanders encountered Kilpatrick's men riding up the mountain.

Site of the Clermont Hotel

Cross over the railroad, and bear to your left at the next sharp curve, and look for hedges on the left of the road. This is where Emack and Capt. Charles Tanner's cannon fell back after their first ambush of Kilpatrick's troops. A stone and brass marking indicates the site of the Clermont Hotel in the hedgerow.

Site of Monterey Hotel

Old Waynesboro Pike becomes Charmian Road. As you approach Monterey Lane (on your left), you will see the location of the old Monterey Hotel, which no longer exists. This was a popular resort before the war, and was Emack's third major defensive position.

Additional Areas of Fighting

Drive another almost half a mile and turn right into the parking lot of the Lion's Club Park. If you walk up the path perpendicular to Charmain Road, you will come to wayside markers explaining the continued fighting between Emack's men and Custer's Wolverines.

The Monterey Park Battlefield Park

The museum is almost across the street from the park, with its back facing Charmian Road. As you make a right turn back onto Charmain Road, you will see the small bridge over Brown's Run. This is where Custer's 1st West Virginia Cavalry and the 1st Ohio Cavalry drove Emack's men back toward the Monterey Pass toll house and started the charge to capture the wagons.

You may wish to visit the museum, open on weekends from April through October.

The Toll House

Continue to the intersection with modern Rt. 16 and cross it. You are now on Old Route 16, the original Emmitsburg-Waynesboro Pike. In about 200 yards, you will see the toll house on the right of the road. This is the original toll house, although it has been expanded and modernized since the fighting. Two Confederate dead (Cpl. William Flowers and Pvt. John Dempster), of the 4th North Carolina Cavalry, were purportedly buried across the street from the toll house. Their bodies were removed in May 1866.

This area saw the Confederates' last stand against Kilpatrick's overwhelming numbers. After driving the enemy cavalry away, Kilpatrick's men captured hundreds of wagons traveling on this road.

As you travel down the hill, toward Rouzerville (called "Waterloo" at the time of the battle), look to the right and see the steep drop off. Imagine the wagons being forced over the side of the mountain from this narrow road.

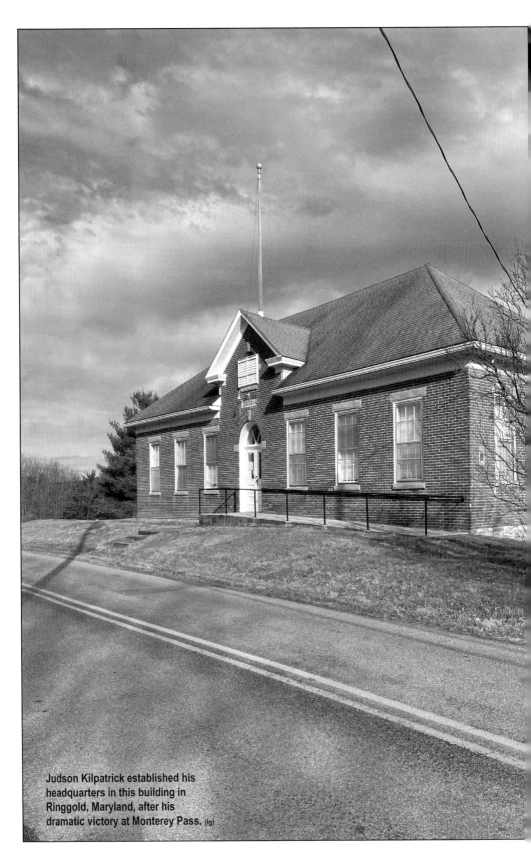

Judson Kilpatrick established his headquarters in this building in Ringgold, Maryland, after his dramatic victory at Monterey Pass. (lg)

Subsequent Cavalry Movements

TOUR C

You may wish to continue the tour, following the path of the cavalry during the remainder of the campaign. This tour follows the route of the cavalry from Rouzerville, Pennsylvania, to Williamsport, Maryland.

Remain on Old Rt. 16 as it heads down the hill into Rouzerville. After a couple of miles from the toll house, the road forks—take the left one, onto Waterloo Road, which becomes Harbaugh Church Road when it crosses Penn Mar Road. Make a left onto Midvale Road/Ringgold Pike (Rt. 418). This is probably close to Kilpatrick's route as he made his way to Smithsburg, Maryland.

After a little more than a mile, you will enter the small village of Ringgold. After his successful raid on Lee's wagon train, Gen. Kilpatrick allowed his men to rest here. Make a left onto Windy Haven Road (Rt. 847). The first building on the left is the old Ringgold School House, where Kilpatrick made his headquarters while his men rested.

Fight at Smithsburg

Union Positions at Smithsburg

Continue on Windy Haven Road, and it will dead end on Rt. 64. Make a left onto it (Smithsburg Pike), and after driving several more miles, turn right onto

Water Street and drive up Gardenhour Hill. Pull over and get out of the car. Face south (toward Rt. 64). The hill you are on was occupied by Col. Pennock Huey's cavalry brigade during the battle of Smithsburg. Brigadier General George Custer's brigade occupied the hill on your left, which now holds the middle school (you will see it later in the tour). Col. Nathaniel Richmond's brigade was on Federal Hill to your right.

Confederate Positions at Smithsburg

You can see South Mountain directly before you. Some Confederate artillery positions were on the high ground (Nicodemus Hill) in the distance. In front of it, you can see Rt. 491, which empties into Rt. 64. This is the road used by Gen. J. E. B. Stuart to approach Smithsburg.

Shell Damage in Smithsburg

Get back into your car and continue driving on Water Street for a third of a mile. You will see the

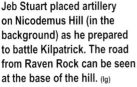

Jeb Stuart placed artillery on Nicodemus Hill (in the background) as he prepared to battle Kilpatrick. The road from Raven Rock can be seen at the base of the hill. (lg)

Leonard Vogel house (25 Water Street) on the right with a Confederate shell embedded in its side (facing you as you pull over). This house and the Bell house (13-15 Water Street) a few doors down the street were used as hospitals during the battle.

A Chicken Meal

Drive another block and make a right onto Main Street. Drive to 42 South Main Street. George Custer and Judson Kilpatrick enjoyed a chicken lunch at this home on the afternoon of July 5, 1863 (between their victory at Monterey Pass and withdrawal from Smithsburg that evening).

The town of Smithfield was hit by Confederate shelling. One such shell can be seen embedded on the side of the Vogel house. (lg)

Custer's Brigade's Position

As you continue driving along Main Street, you will pass the Middle School on the right, the location of Custer's brigade's position during the "battle" of Smithsburg.

Battle of Hagerstown

Hagerstown

Kilpatrick's cavalry left Smithsburg on the evening of July 5 and rode to Boonsboro. They then went north to Hagerstown the following day, where they again battled Stuart's cavalry. We will be visiting Boonsboro during the Union infantry tour. Now, we will take the fastest route to Hagerstown.

We need to turn around and return the way we came. This can be accomplished by pulling into the school's parking lot. Get back on Main Street and travel to Water Street, which becomes Mapleville Road (Rt. 66). At the intersection with Rt. 64 (traffic light), make a right and drive about six miles to Hagerstown. The road dead ends, so you must make a right onto Cannon, and then a left onto N. Potomac Street.

Zion Reformed Church of Christ

You will see this church on the right as you travel almost a mile. This church was established in 1770 and was used by Confederates during the battle on July 6, who fired from behind its stout stone walls and from the church's cemetery. As you drive down the street, imagine civilians at their windows facing Potomac Street, firing at the Confederate troopers.

Drive down the hill, and at its base is the approximate spot where Capt. Ulric Dahlgren received a grievous leg wound as he led a portion of the 18th Pennsylvania Cavalry against a stubborn Confederate resistance.

Continue driving south on Potomac Street to Baltimore Street, where the 10th Virginia erected one of its barricades.

Make a left on Baltimore Street and drive a couple of blocks to a "Y." Bear to your right onto Frederick Street (Alternate 40). The high ground on your left, just beyond the intersection, was occupied by Union horse artillery during the battle.

Continue on Frederick Street to East Memorial Blvd. If you wish to see the Rose Hill Cemetery, turn right onto E. Memorial Blvd to the cemetery gatehouse. Turn into the cemetery and take the first road to the right to the "Confederate Cemetery" within Rose Hill Cemetery. There are very few gravestones here, although it contains hundreds of graves. One

The Washington Confederate Cemetery within Hagerstown's Rose Hill Cemetery was established in 1871 to bury the Confederate dead from the Antietam battlefield and those who died in Maryland during the retreat from Gettysburg. Colonel Isaac Avery is among the dead buried here. He died at Gettysburg and his body was transported to Williamsport, then ultimately buried here. (lg)

of those marked is that of Col. Isaac Avery, who was killed during the battle of Gettysburg. His slave initially brought his body to Williamsport, where it was buried, but later moved to the Confederate Cemetery in Hagerstown.

If you visit the cemetery, backtrack toward Frederick Street, and turn right. If you did not visit the cemetery, continue on Frederick Street (Alt. Rt. 40) toward Funkstown. At the traffic circle, take the N. Westside Avenue exit, cross over Antietam Creek on the stone bridge, and turn right onto E. Oak Ridge Drive. Park in the American Legion parking lot on your right.

Battle of Funkstown

Infantry Movements

The stone bridge you see spanning Antietam Creek was used by Confederate infantry to reinforce Jeb Stuart's cavalry, who were initially fighting John Buford's men on July 10. Longstreet's troops occupied the area on the west side of the bridge.

Exit the parking lot by making a left turn on E. Oak Ridge Drive, and drive a block to West Baltimore Street (Alt. 40). Continue east on Baltimore Street through Funkstown.

Homes That Played a Role in the Battle of Funkstown

The Davis house (29 West Baltimore) on the right was owned by Angela Davis, a New Yorker by birth, who lived here with her husband and cared for both Union and Confederate wounded in her home after the battle. West Baltimore Street becomes East Baltimore Street, and you will see period homes on either side. Maj. H. D. McDaniel of the 11th Georgia Infantry was laid in front of the Keller house (24 E. Baltimore Street), which is on the left side of the street, before being taken inside for medical attention. He survived the war and became governor of Georgia. Directly across the street is the Hudson house, which was also used as a hospital after the battle. A bit further

Like so many buildings in Funkstown, the Keller house was used as a hospital. Major H. D. McDaniel of the 11th Georgia Infantry was treated here. The house was built around the start of the Civil War. (lg)

up the street, the Chaney house (41 East Baltimore) was also used as a field hospital.

Fighting Outside of Funkstown

Continue on East Baltimore Street out of town. It becomes Beaver Creek Road. You may not see a sign with that name, but simply stay on the road. The road forks with Hebb Road—stay right on Beaver Creek Road. Set your odometer to zero, and at 0.4 miles, you will come to low ground on your right. Georgians from Brig. Gen. George Anderson's brigade were in this area, attacking the high ground in front of you occupied by Union troops.

John Buford's Cavalry Arrive

Continue driving, and you will arrive at the intersection with Emmert Road. If you look to the right, along Emmert Road, you will see the route that John Buford's cavalry and the Vermont Brigade took to reach this area from Boonsboro. Behind you, Jeb Stuart had initially deployed his men in a semi-circle around Funkstown.

Union Infantry/Artillery Positions

Make a left onto Emmert Road. Later during the action, Col. Lewis Grant's Vermont Brigade relieved Buford's men, and formed along Emmert Road. This high ground was also occupied by Union artillery.

Buford's Headquarters

Continue driving on Emmert Road for about 0.5 miles to Hebb Road (just before an intersection with a major road), and carefully turn left onto it. The J. W. Baker farm (102 Hebb Road) is on the right, after about a quarter-mile drive. This was the site of John Buford's headquarters during the battle. Behind the farm, you can see the high ground that was occupied by Union troops during the battle.

Continue driving along Hebb Road, which becomes Beaver Creek Road and then East Baltimore Street. Make a left onto Frederick Road (Alternate Route 40). As you approach I-70, you will see a parking area on your right. Pull in and read the historical markers.

Jeb Stuart's Position

Across the street, you will see the old Hauck barn. This area was occupied by Jeb Stuart's cavalry, and later by Georgia infantry, during the battle of Funkstown.

Williamsport

Backtrack toward Funkstown and make a left onto Baltimore Street, which becomes East Oak Ridge Drive after you cross Antietam Creek. Drive around the traffic circle and continue on East Oak Ridge Drive. Take this road to Rt. 65 (traffic light) and make a left onto it. You will pass under I-70, and after driving a few miles, you will come to College Road. Make a right onto it.

The exclusive St. James College was founded as a preparatory school in 1842. It continues to educate youth as one of 24 Episcopal schools in the U.S. (lg)

St. James School
Drive through the school's campus, and after 2.2 miles you will see a green fence boarding an athletic field. Pull over and look to your right to see the high ground on which Imboden laid out his defensive line composed of cavalry and artillery. Look to your left and see the ground used by Col. William Gamble to attack this skirmish line on July 6. Look ahead and to your right, and you will see the area attacked by Company F, 21st Virginia Infantry that stopped Gamble's advance, but at the cost of Capt. William Pegram's life.

John Buford's Headquarters
Continue driving on College Road until you reach Lappans Road. Make a right onto this road and drive two miles to Kendle Road, and turn right. After almost a mile, you will see the Elmwood Farm (16311 Kendle Road) on your left, Gen. John Buford's headquarters during the Williamsport fight on July 6.

Imboden's Wagons
Turn around and make a right onto Lappens Road, which takes you into Williamsport. The town of Williamsport has grown, destroying much of the

battleground around it. Lappans Road becomes N. Conococheague Street after you pass under I-81. A bit further on it becomes S. Conococheague Street. After a few blocks, make a left onto West Potomac Street, and follow the signs to the C&O National Historic Park. Park your car in the lot, and walk along the canal to the elevated crossing, which takes you to the low ground between the Potomac River and the canal. This is where Gen. Imboden parked thousands of wagons, axle to axle, until the water receded enough for the wagons and men to cross the river. Walk to the river and look at the bridge over it, and you will see the approximate location of one of the fords. A second ford was about 200 yards further upriver to your right.

Falling Waters

Backtrack the way you came to Lappans Road. After you pass beneath I-81, you will see a sign to Governor Lane Boulevard on the left. Ignore it and instead make a right onto Spielman Road (Rt. 63). After a couple of miles, turn right onto Falling Waters Road and drive almost three miles to the Daniel Donnelly house. This is privately owned, so please do

James Pettigrew's and James Archer's brigades (Heth's division) assumed a defensive position in this field as the rest of Lee's army crossed the Potomac River. It has been protected from future development. (lg)

Not everyone believes in battlefield preservation. This sign on the field across the street from Pettigrew's and Archer's positions is owned by a family who will not consider selling it to ensure its future preservation. (lg)

not park in the driveway. It is best to park along the road before you reach it.

Confederate Rearguard

Look to the right, and you will see a Falling Waters preservation sign. This is the position occupied by James Archer's and James Pettigrew's brigades during the rearguard action on July 14. Colonel John Brockenbrough's and Gen. Joseph Davis' brigades were deployed across the road, on land that is unpreserved. These units were initially attacked by the elements of the 6th Michigan led by Maj. Peter Weber on the morning of July 14 as the rest of Lee's army was crossing the Potomac River.

Donnally House

The house was built in 1815 and was surrounded by the swirling battle on July 14. A small shed beyond the right of the house is supposed to be the approximate location of the barn that concealed a Union trooper who shot and mortally wounded Gen. Pettigrew during the fight.

Road to the Ford

Get back into your car and drive to the gate and the sign for the Potomac Fish and Game Club, Inc. You can see an old road beyond the gate, the continuation of Falling Waters Road used by Longstreet's and then Hill's corps to reach the pontoon bridge spanning the Potomac River. Despite what you may have heard, this is private land, and you should not enter this property.

This ends the tour. You can backtrack your steps to Rt. 81.

The owner of the Black Horse Tavern also owned Bream's Hill, just to the east. Lee purportedly sat on his horse at the top of the hill as his troops trudged past. (lg)

Lee's Army Retreats

TOUR D

This route follows the path of Lee's army from Gettysburg to Hagerstown. The army was preceded by Maj. John Harman's reserve wagon train and Ewell's ambulances and wagon train.

The tour begins at the Gettysburg Theological Seminary.

Bream's Hill

Turn right onto Fairfield Road and drive 1.8 miles to Bream's Hill Road. This is the original trace of Fairfield Road. The road was straightened after the war, but this part remains. Make a right onto the road and carefully stop at the top of the hill (Herr's Ridge Road is coming in from the right). The latter road was used by many of Ewell's wagons and ambulances that had been traveling along Fairfield Road. Longstreet's ambulances were sent to the Cashtown Road by this road. Lee purportedly halted his horse here on the evening of July 4 and watched his troops' slow progress toward Fairfield. Major Jed Hotchkiss and his topographical engineers were also present, in a wagon copying maps showing the route to Williamsport.

Black Horse Tavern

Drive a third of a mile to the Black Horse Tavern site on the right. The tavern was owned by Francis Bream at the time of the battle, hence the name of the

One of many establishments used by the Confederates as a hospital west and north of town, the Black Horse Tavern was built in 1812 by Francis Bream. It is currently a private residence. (lg)

hill beyond it. The wounded and sick of Brig. Gen. Joseph Kershaw's brigades (Lafayette McLaws's division) filled the house and massive bank barn, one of the largest in the county. About 220 wounded were left behind with three surgeons when the army evacuated. As many as 70 men were buried in the yard of the property.

Granite Hill

Drive another 2.6 miles and see a ridge called "Granite Hill." Brigadier General Albion Howe's division was deployed across this hill with supporting artillery. At the top of the hill, you will see another hill in the distance. This is the Confederate position, manned by the 26th Georgia (Gordon's Brigade) and some artillery. Fighting occurred along Muddy Run between the two hills.

Carroll's Tract Road

After driving almost two miles from Granite Hill, you will see a road coming in from the right (at the post office). There was a small Confederate hospital operating here. This road leads to Cashtown, and along this road Lee had amassed his wagons and livestock. Harman's long wagon train moved down this road to Fairfield Road to begin the long return trip to Virginia.

Iron Springs Road

Drive through Fairfield, and after a bit more than a mile, turn right onto Iron Springs Road. Before you do, you will see Jack's Mountain in front of you and the narrow Fairfield Gap to your right. James Longstreet's First Corps and its wagons left the column here, and continued marching straight, over the mountain on Jack's Mountain Road, emerging on the Emmitsburg-Waynesboro Turnpike (see the beginning of the Monterey Tour for additional information).

We will follow Harman's reserve wagons, Hill's and Ewell's corps, and their wagons, which made a right onto Iron Springs Road from Fairfield Road. You will see Tom's Creek on either side of the road as you drive along Iron Spring Road, and remnants of the "Tapeworm Railroad," an aborted project that was pushed by Thaddeus Stevens.

After around three miles, turn right onto Gum Springs Road. The roads were becoming very muddy as rain deluged this area, and thousands of wagons used them. After driving a few miles, near the top of South Mountain, you will see the trace of Maria Furnace Road (near mailbox 11225). Lee's wagons used this road to reach Monterey Pass.

You will pass the stone Benchooff house on your left, just over three miles after you turn onto Gum Springs Road. As Lee passed by this house, he was invited by local ladies to join them for tea, which was served on a large rock in the yard.

On your left, you will see the Old Waynesboro Road. During the time of the battle, this formed part of the Emmitsburg-Waynesboro Pike. Judson Kilpatrick's division rode up the mountain on this road toward Monterey Pass (ahead of you). A day later, Longstreet used this road to reach the pass.

You will drive through the quaint village of Charmain, which was a popular vacation spot because of the clean mountain air. As you approach Monterey Lane, the large Monterey Springs Hotel would have been on your left. It is gone now, essentially without a trace.

The road from Emmitsburg to Waynesboro was a turnpike that did not follow the same route as the modern Rt. 16. The toll house still stands but has been expanded through the years. (lg)

Two large rocks can be seen in the yard of the Benschoff house. The one with the flat top in the rear was probably used by the ladies who served Robert E. Lee during the retreat. (lg)

Toll House

After crossing modern Rt. 16, the road name changes to Old Route 16, and within 200 yards you will see the toll house on the right.

Lee's Rock

Drive a quarter mile beyond the toll house to a large flat rock on the left side of the road. This is "Lee's Rock #2" and was used by the army leader to give a short inspirational speech to his officers. A resident, Samuel Wallace, heard the speech and noted how Lee mentioned some of the officers lost in the recent battle and his concern for his army's safety as it headed back to Virginia.

Lee purportedly stood on this rock just down the road from the Monterey Pass toll house, encouraging his men as they marched past. (lg)

Two Additional Graves

As you drive several miles down the mountain, you will come to 12128 Old Route 16 on the left side of the road. Legend has it that two other Confederate soldiers were buried at this location. No one knows whether these bodies still rest in their shallow graves.

Continue driving down Old Rt. 16 until the road forks. This is the location of the Buena Vista stagecoach stop. Stay on Old Rt. 16, which is the right fork. There is another fork with Waterloo Road, but stay right on Old Route 16. At the modern Rt. 16 traffic light, make a left onto it.

Stephey Tavern

Near the intersection of the old and new Rt. 16 stood the former site of the Stephey Tavern on the left side of the road. Lee stopped here during the retreat for a meal. The house was once the home of Peter Rouzer, the founder of Rouzerville, but was leveled and removed in 2007.

To Rouzerville and Waynesboro

Continue traveling through Rouzerville (called "Pikesville" at the time of the battle) toward downtown Waynesboro. You will pass a hospital on your right. During the retreat, David Hoeflich owned a house here. Many marching soldiers gave the house a wide berth because hives of angry bees patrolled the area.

Continue into Waynesboro. Townspeople came out to watch Lee ride through the town's main street, and two field hospitals were established in the town. One was a few blocks down on Cottage Street (at the intersection with Middle Street). Many townspeople took to their gardens to "plant" valuables as Lee's men passed.

The Waynesboro Town Square

Not much of the town square remains, but it was at the intersection of Main and Church Streets. Legend has it that Lee stopped at the public water pump to allow his horse, Traveller, to drink while he conversed with his aides.

To Leitersburg and Hagerstown

Lee took the direct route to the two Maryland towns. Follow his route by making a left turn on S. Potomac Street, and drive about five miles southwest on Rt. 60 to Leitersburg. While approaching the town on the Leitersburg-Hagerstown Pike, Lee passed many of his wagons destroyed by the 1st Vermont Cavalry. He and the column continued onto Hagerstown, his final destination, since the ford at Williamsport and the pontoon bridge at Falling Waters were no longer available.

Remain on Potomac Street as you drive through Hagerstown. Lee's defensive line on Salisbury Ridge was west of the town. You will drive under I-70 and travel about two and a half miles to the traffic light at College Street.

Follow Tour C for Williamsport/ Falling Waters/ Salisbury Ridge.

Devil's backbone park is a popular recreational area. During the Gettysburg Campaign, it occupied roughly the center of Meade's line. (lg)

The Union Army's Pursuit

TOUR E

The Union army took several routes from Gettysburg to reach its rallying point at Middletown, Maryland. Therefore, our tour will begin in the latter town, but you may wish to follow a tour from Gettysburg.

The I, III, and VI Corps:
Emmitsburg, Mechanicstown, Lewistown, Hamburg, to Middletown

The V and XI Corps:
Emmitsburg, Creagerstown, Utica, Highknob Pass to Middletown

The II and XII Corps:
Taneytown, Middleburg, Woodsborough, Frederick to Middletown

Middletown

Begin the tour at Middletown, Maryland. Five of the seven corps (I, III, V, VI, XI) made their way to South Mountain and crossed over it at Turner's Gap. The other two corps (II and XII) swung south to cross at Crampton's Gap. We will follow the route of the majority of the army.

Main Street runs through the middle of Middletown. Drive west through Middletown on West Main Street (Rt. 40, alternate). This is the original National Highway. As you leave Middletown, you will see South Mountain looming ahead. You will cross over the mountain using Turner's Gap, which was the scene of intense fighting during the Maryland Campaign. It was undefended during the Gettysburg Campaign. After crossing South Mountain, you will reach Boonsboro and drive through it.

Cavalry Fight at Boonsboro

After leaving Boonsboro, you will pass Rt. 68 on your left. Continue less than a mile to the "Auction Square Market Place" on your left and pull into their parking lot. This is where Stuart's cavalry battled Kilpatrick's and Buford's divisions outside of Boonsboro on July 8. The matter was settled when units from the VI and XI infantry corps marched through Boonsboro after traversing Turner's Gap to support the Union cavalry. Stuart wisely withdrew and headed back north to Funkstown.

Devil's Backbone County Park

Make a right turn back onto Alt. Rt. 40 and then, within a mile, make a right onto Rt. 68 (Lappans Road). Cross the stone bridge over Antietam Creek, and turn right into the park's parking lot. Look across the road at the houses. One of these may have been George Meade's headquarters on July 10. Meade held an important Council of War here on the evening of July 12 to determine whether he had support for an attack on Lee's entrenched position on Salisbury Ridge.

Jones' Crossroads

Make a right turn out of the parking lot and continue on Lappans Road. You will come to an intersection (with Rt. 65) that has a traffic light, and is known as Jones' Crossroads. This area was important because Gens. Buford and Kilpatrick met here after dark on July 6— after each had experienced setbacks that day. On July 11, portions of Col. Pennock Huey's cavalry brigade and some elements of the XII Corps skirmished with Confederate infantry and cavalry after dark.

General Slocum's Headquarters

Make a left on Rt. 65 (Sharpsburg Pike), and after about 0.7 miles, you will see a white farmhouse on the right. This was Gen. Henry Slocum's XII Corps headquarters. A little further ahead, you would be on the left flank of Meade's army.

This old farmhouse was used by Maj. Gen. Henry Slocum of the XII Corps while Lee's army was pinned against the Potomac River. It was probably in considerably better shape than it is today. (lg)

The Rest of Meade's Line

Carefully make a U-turn and continue north on Rt. 65. Meade's line ran along this road—in some cases, the infantry units were to the left of the road, in other cases, on the right. The line extended just north of Funkstown, but there is little to see if you follow this route.

College of St. James

At the traffic signal at Jones' Crossroads, if you continue north on Lappans Road (Route 68), you will come to College Road. Turn right into College Road and the College of Saint James is ahead on your right. Just before the College are the fields on each side of the road where Buford's troops skirmished with Confederate cavalry and artillery on July 6 when Buford was heading to Williamsport to capture the Confederate wagons. Buford's troops encountered Confederate wagons forging for hay and wheat. They stopped the wagons, setting them on fire. The mules and teamsters panicked as the flames engulfed the wagons.

Confederate Line of Defense

Turn around and backtrack to Lappans Road. Turn right on Lappans Road, and continue to the next traffic signal at the intersection of Lappans Road and Downsville Pike (Route 632). If you go left on the Downsville Pike, you will be following Salisbury Ridge and the defense line of the Confederates occupied by Longstreet. If you turn right, you will be close to the Confederate defense line extending to just west of Hagerstown. Hill's Corps was in the middle and Ewell was near Hagerstown. If you continue north on Lappans Road, you will be at Williamsport.

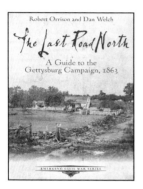

The Last Road North: A Guide to the Gettysburg Campaign, 1863
Robert Orrison and Dan Welch
Savas Beatie, 2016
ISBN-13: 978-1611212433

This book in the Emerging Civil War Series offers tours that follow the Confederate and U.S. armies to Gettysburg, a tour that follows Jeb Stuart's cavalry, and a tour that follows the armies' race to the Potomac River. Built around a number of Civil War Trails sites, each tour offers detailed directions.

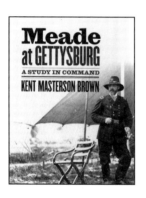

Meade at Gettysburg: A Study in Command
Kent Masterson Brown
University of North Carolina Press, 2021
ISBN-13: 978-1469661995

An in-depth analysis of Meade's leadership during the Gettysburg Campaign. Brown spends considerable time explaining why Meade pursued Lee's army as he did.

Retreat from Gettysburg: Lee, Logistics, and the Pennsylvania Campaign
Kent Masterson Brown
University of North Carolina Press, 2005
ISBN-10: 0807829218

A masterful review of Lee's retreat from Gettysburg. Brown plows new ground by explaining the immense amount of foraging by Lee's army during its retreat.

The Maps of Gettysburg: An Atlas of the Gettysburg Campaign, June 3–July 13, 1863
Bradley M. Gottfried
Savas Beatie, 2007
ISBN: 978-1932714821

Reviews the campaign in many full-color maps. A considerable portion of the book covers the post-Gettysburg events.

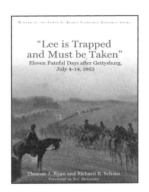

The Maps of the Cavalry in the Gettysburg Campaign
Bradley M. Gottfried
Savas Beatie, 2020
ISBN: 978-1611214796

Addresses the often under-appreciated role of the cavalry in all phases of the Gettysburg Campaign. The book is filled with full-color maps of the action.

"Lee is Trapped and Must be Taken": Eleven Fateful Days after Gettysburg, July 4–14, 1863
Thomas J. Ryan and Richard R. Schaus
Savas Beatie, 2019
ISBN-13: 978-1611214598

A wonderful overview of Lee's retreat and Meade's pursuit. The authors do not hesitate in interpreting the effectiveness of each army's leaders.

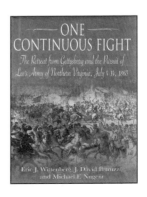

One Continuous Fight: The Retreat from Gettysburg and the Pursuit of Lee's Army of Northern Virginia, July 4–14, 1863
Eric J. Wittenberg, J. David Petruzzi, and Michael F. Nugent
Savas Beatie, 2008
ISBN-13: 978-1932714432

Although this book covers the entire post-Gettysburg campaign, it concentrates on the cavalry actions.

About the Authors

Bradley M. Gottfried served as a college educator for more than 40 years before retiring in 2017. After receiving his doctorate, he worked as a full-time faculty member before entering the administrator ranks. He rose to the position of president and served for 17 years at two colleges. His interest in the Civil War began when he was a youngster in the Philadelphia area. He has written 18 books on the Civil War, including a number on Gettysburg as well as map studies of various campaigns. A resident of the Chambersburg/Gettysburg, Pennsylvania area, Brad is an Antietam Licensed Battlefield Guide and a Gettysburg Licensed Town Guide.

Linda I. Gottfried served as a graphic designer and development officer at several colleges and nonprofit organizations before retiring in 2015. She is now a full-time sculptor. Several of her pieces have won awards.

Brad and Linda have collaborated on three projects: *Hell Comes to Southern Maryland* (published by Turning Point Publications), *Lincoln Comes to Gettysburg: The Creation of the Soldiers' National Cemetery and Lincoln's Gettysburg Address* (published by Savas Beatie as part of the Emerging Civil War Series), and *The Antietam Paintings of James B. Hope* (published by Turning Point Publications).

The Gottfrieds live in Fayetteville, Pennsylvania, and have five children and seven grandchildren.